Chloe's Kitchen

125 Easy, Delicious Recipes for Making the Food You Love the Vegan Way

CHLOE COSCARELLI

Foreword by Neal D. Barnard, M.D.

FREE PRESS

New York   London   Toronto   Sydney   New Delhi

FREE PRESS
A Division of Simon & Schuster, Inc.
1230 Avenue of the Americas
New York, NY 10020

First Free Press trade paperback edition March 2012

FREE PRESS and colophon are trademarks of Simon & Schuster, Inc.

For information about special discounts for bulk purchases,
please contact Simon & Schuster Special Sales at 1-866-506-1949
or business@simonandschuster.com.

The Simon & Schuster Speakers Bureau can bring authors to your live event.
For more information or to book an event, contact the Simon & Schuster Speakers Bureau
at 1-866-248-3049 or visit our website at www.simonspeakers.com.

Manufactured in the United States of America

1   3   5   7   9   10   8   6   4   2

Library of Congress Cataloging-in-Publication Data
Coscarelli, Chloe.
Chloe's kitchen : 125 easy, delicious recipes for making the food you love the vegan way /
Chloe Coscarelli ; foreword by Neal D. Barnard.—
1st ed.
p. cm.
Includes index.
1. Vegan cooking. 2. Cookbooks. I. Title.
TX837.C664 2012
641.5'636—dc23
2011050694

ISBN 978-1-4516-3674-1
ISBN 978-1-4516-3675-8 (ebook)

■

To my best friend,
my mom,
for teaching me how to cook
and encouraging me
to follow my dreams.
I love you.

■

Contents

Introduction   xi
Foreword   xv
Vegan Pantry   1
Gluten-Free and Soy-Free Cooking   11

Small Bites   13
Artichoke-Walnut Pesto Crostini   15
Avocado-Shiitake Sushi   16
Balsamic Bruschetta   19
Black Bean Baby Cakes with Pineapple Salsa   20
Crispy Potato-Leek Patties with Lemon-Dill Dip   22
Garlic Knots   25
Garlic White Bean Dip   27
Kalamata Olive Tapenade   27
Jalapeño Cornbread Poppers with Whipped Maple Butter   29
Mini Potato Skins Stuffed with Avocado Salsa   31
Sweet-and-Sour Party Meatballs   33
Phyllo Mushroom Turnovers   36
Samosas with Cilantro-Tamarind Dipping Sauce   38
Warm Spinach-Artichoke Dip   41
Wontons with Apricot-Mustard Sauce   43

Soups and Salads   45
Caesar Salad with Maple-Wheat Croutons   47
California Chipotle Chop with Agave-Lime Vinaigrette   49
Cheesy Broccoli Soup in Sourdough Bread Bowls   51
Chloe's Favorite Five-Minute Salad   53
Curried Lentil, Squash, and Apple Stew   55
Easy Peasy Pasta Salad   57
Mandarin Peanut-Crunch Salad with Crispy Wontons   59
Minted Couscous with Arugula, Butternut Squash, and Currants   61
Simple Side Salad with Shallot-Dijon Vinaigrette   62

Tomato-Basil Bisque with Pumpernickel Croutons   63

Tuscan Bean and Greens Soup over Garlic Toast   66

Wasabi Sesame Noodle Salad   68

Simply Vegetables   69

Classic Roasted Vegetables   71

Coconut Mashed Yams with Currants   73

Fire-Roasted Artichokes with Garlic Oil   75

Garlicky Greens   77

Grilled Lemon–Olive Oil Asparagus   78

Guilt-Free Garlic Mashed Potatoes   79

Maple-Roasted Brussels Sprouts with Toasted Hazelnuts   81

Teriyaki Wok Vegetables   83

Miso-Glazed Eggplant   85

Sea Salt and Vinegar French Fries   87

Thyme for Creamy Scalloped Potatoes   89

Vegetable Tempura   91

Under-the-Sea Vegetables   92

Eat with Your Hands   93

Avocado Toast   95

BBQ Pineapple Pizza   97

Grilled Pesto Pizza with Sweet Potatoes, Kale, and Balsamic Reduction   98

Chloe's Award-Winning Mango Masala Panini   101

Double Double Drive-Thru Burgers   103

Falafel Sliders with Avocado Hummus   107

LA-Style Chimichurri Tacos   109

Moo Shu Vegetables with Homemade Chinese Pancakes   113

Portobello Pesto Panini   116

Rosemary Tomato Galette with Pine Nut Ricotta   117

Thai Chickpea Burgers with Sweet 'n' Spicy Sauce   121

Oodles of Noodles   123

Avocado Pesto Pasta   125

Best-Ever Baked Macaroni and Cheese   127

Chinese Takeout Chow Mein   129

Orecchiette in No-Cook Spinach Sauce   131
Drunken Noodles in Cashew-Shiitake Broth   133
Fettuccine Alfredo   135
Ooh-La-La Lasagna   136
Pasta Italiano   138
Peanutty Perfection Noodles   141
Penne alla Vodka with the Best Garlic Bread in the World   143
Spaghetti Bolognese   145
Straw and Hay Pasta   147
Stuffed Shells with Arrabbiata Sauce   149
Sweet Potato Gnocchi with Sage Butter   151
Wild Mushroom Stroganoff Fettuccine   155

The Main Event   **157**
Barley Bliss Casserole   158
Caribbean Vegetables with Coconut Rice and Plantains   159
Country Meatloaf and Golden Gravy with Orange-Scented Cranberry Sauce   161
Eggplant Timbales   165
Green Curry Crepes   168
Herbed Polenta Cutlets with Marsala Mushroom Ragout   170
Indian Buffet Trio: Saag Aloo, Chana Masala, and Vegetable Biryani,
    with Garlic Naan   172
Mongolian BBQ Seitan   177
Moroccan Bistilla   179
Orange You Glad I Made Crispy Tofu?   181
Pancakes for Dinner   183
Pineapple Not-So-Fried Rice   185
Seitan Scallopini   186
Southern Skillet Black-Eyed Peas with Quick Buttery Biscuits   187
Tempeh Piccata   191
Tropical Island Kebabs with Cilantro Rice   193

Cupcakes and More   **195**
Baked Sprinkle Doughnuts   197
Banana Cupcakes with Lemon Icing   199
Chloe's Award-Winning Ginger Nutmeg Spice Cupcakes   201

"Chlostess" Crème-Filled Cupcakes   205

Chocolate Chip Brownie Bites   207

Buckeyes   209

Chocolate Crème Brûlée   210

Chocolate Molten Lava Cakes with Raspberry Sauce   213

Happy Birthday Cake   215

Chocolate Walnut Fudge   219

Cinnamon-Espresso Chocolate Chip Cookies   221

Hot Fudge Sundaes with Mint Chip Ice Cream   223

Iced Apple Cake Squares   225

Mocha Almond Fudge Cake   227

Ooey Gooey Cinnamon Rolls   229

Sea Salt Toffee Bars   233

Summer Berry Pie à La Mode   235

Vanilla Bean Ice Cream   238

Tarte Tatin with Coconut Whipped Cream   239

Truffles   243

Yoga Cookies   245

Peanut Butter Dog Treats   247

The Basics   249

Basic Pizza Dough   250

Beans and Grains   251

Homemade Seitan   252

Pressing Tofu   252

Sweet Tomato Ketchup   253

Sour Cream   254

Barbecue Sauce   254

Marinara Sauce   255

Sweet-and-Sour Sauce   256

Soy-Free Soy Sauce   257

Toasting Nuts   257

Menu Suggestions   259

Acknowledgments   263

Index   265

Introduction

You can cook!

For the first eighteen years of my life, I genuinely believed I couldn't cook. I didn't think I had the patience, skills, or palate for cooking, all because of a couple less-than-perfect attempts. Guess what I learned? With a little bit of practice and a good appetite, anyone and everyone can cook. That means you!

What the heck is this vegan cooking thing?

This is the question I get asked the most. Vegan cooking is preparing food without any ingredients that come from animals. No meat, poultry, fish, dairy, or eggs. Vegan (or plant-based) food is naturally low in fat, cholesterol free, and more healthful than meat or butter-laden foods. If you think I'm talking about sprout sandwiches and bland tofu, think again! These pages are filled with flavor-loaded, moist and juicy, ooey-gooey, party-in-your-mouth recipes that no one will ever believe are vegan. You can make elegant and mouth-watering meals that will leave you feeling satisfied and energized without using any animal products. Vegan food is healing for your body, great for the planet, and much easier to prepare than you think!

Living on the Veg

I've always been a huge animal lover. You name it, I've adopted it. From pit bulls and rats to frogs and lizards, I've always been a please-can-we-keep-him? kind of girl. One day, in seventh grade, I made the connection between the pets I loved and the food on my plate. It suddenly didn't make sense for me to eat animals for dinner then cuddle with my pups at night. I decided to become a vegetarian, and I went vegan a few years later. My meat-eating, yet open-minded and supportive family soon followed my living-on-the-veg lead. My mom went crazy in the kitchen, veganizing every passed-down family recipe in her repertoire for us, and she urged me to join her in the fun. Before I knew it, I was learning how to cook with her, eating delicious new foods, losing weight, and feeling great.

Aha Moments, Oven Lights, and the Big Apple

Everyone talks about having an *aha* moment; you know, when the oven light in your head clicks on. For me, this happened in college at UC Berkeley. I was studying sociology and dance and living with five fabulous girls in a tiny apartment with a kitchen no bigger than a car. I spent more hours than I could ever count in that kitchen. My friends and I pulled many all-nighters studying for exams, but I would always make time for baking elaborate triple-tiered birthday cakes for my roommates and throwing buffet-style brunch parties on Sunday mornings. Nothing gave me more joy than cooking and baking, and I realized that I wanted to spend my life doing just that. *Aha!*

Right after graduation, I packed up my knives and whisks and hopped on a plane to New York City to attend culinary school at The Natural Gourmet Institute. It ended up being the most incredible experience of my life. Sure, there were onion tears, burns, cuts, and tomato-sauce stains along the way, but we all know that the most difficult experiences are the most rewarding.

Cupcake Wars

I saw a casting call for a new Food Network competition show, *Cupcake Wars*, and auditioned on a whim. Before I knew it, I was on the show, pitted against three other talented, nonvegan pastry chefs, all of whom had butter, cream, and eggs in their arsenals. Among the judges was pastry superstar Candace Nelson, founder of the world's first cupcake bakery, Sprinkles Cupcakes. No turning back—it was time for a sweet smackdown for cupcake supremacy!

I enlisted the assistance of my brilliant medical-school-bound college roommate, Sandhya Jacob, who doesn't buckle under pressure and is a cake decorating rock star. Neither of us knew what to expect, but there is nothing more thrilling than taking a risk with your best friend by your side.

We mustered every ounce of our creativity, baked our hearts out, and one thousand cupcakes later, took home first prize. The judges loved every bite of my frosting-topped masterpieces and couldn't believe they were vegan. At that moment I realized that my mom's age-old advice was true: Believe in yourself, never give up, and anything is possible . . . *Anything!*

So, let's get cooking!

At last! Here it is: my heart and soul in the form of a cookbook. I am so excited to be sharing my sweet and savory recipes with you and so touched that you are trying them. Enjoy them with your family, your friends, or your beautiful self. Get creative and add your own spicy touch. Let loose and have fun! In a hurry? Take a shortcut. No time to chop? Buy cut veggies at your local grocery store. Don't have fresh thyme? Try it with-

out or use dried. The conversion is 1 teaspoon dried to 1 tablespoon fresh herbs. Added too much salt? Counteract it with a splash of lemon juice. Trust yourself to create solutions to any obstacle you encounter in the kitchen—that's when the fun begins.

If you have any questions along the way, you can visit my online community at ChefChloe.com to get helpful cooking tips, connect with other food lovers, or simply say hello.

Live, Dream, Eat,

Chloe

Foreword

If you want to lose weight, reduce cholesterol, and boost your energy, you've opened the right book. Many studies, including some from the Physicians Committee for Responsible Medicine, have shown that when people switch to a plant-based diet and cut out greasy animal fats, they can shed unwanted pounds and gain vitality. The health benefits of a plant-based diet are enormous, and Chloe makes this way of cooking easy, accessible, and extremely flavorful. Before you get cooking, you may be wondering how a vegan diet will affect your body. Will you get enough protein? Is it healthy for kids? These are great questions that are asked all the time, so let's jump right in and set some facts straight about plant-based nutrition.

Will I lose weight?

Yes, if you have weight to lose. If you're already at your ideal weight, you'll stay there. However, if you are carrying excess weight, a plant-based diet is the way to go. When you build your meals from vegetables, fruits, whole grains, and beans, and keep oils to a minimum, weight loss is remarkably easy. Chloe has put together a creative array of easy-to-follow, delicious, plant-based recipes that will leave you feeling healthier, lighter, and more energized. If you are ready to try this way of eating, let me encourage you to really give it a good, solid try. You'll find it easier not only to lose weight but also to maintain a healthy weight permanently. No more yo-yo dieting!

Many people think that carbohydrates like pasta, bread, potatoes, and rice are fattening. This is not true, unless you're slathering fat on them, like butter on bread, or meat sauce on spaghetti. Carbohydrates actually have fewer than half the calories of fat, which means that replacing fatty foods with complex carbohydrates automatically cuts calories. The most effective weight-control programs use a high-complex carbohydrate, low-fat, vegan diet, along with regular exercise.

Will I get enough protein?

Yes, absolutely. As long as you're eating a variety of plant foods—grains, beans, vegetables, and fruits—in sufficient quantity, as Chloe outlines in this book, you'll get plenty of protein. No special food combining is necessary.

Does a plant-based diet fight illnesses such as cancer, diabetes, and heart disease?
In 1990, Dr. Dean Ornish showed that a vegetarian diet, along with other lifestyle changes, can reverse heart disease. Our work shows that people with type 2 diabetes often improve to the point that they need less medication or can even come off their medication completely. Many studies have shown that cancer is less common among people who follow predominantly plant-based diets. This diet has also been proven helpful even after cancer is diagnosed.

Is a plant-based diet healthy for my children?
The answer is yes, and Chloe shares a ton of tasty, kid-friendly recipes such as vegan macaroni and cheese, tacos, and kale-topped pizza. A plant-based diet is much better for children than a diet that includes animal-based products. The rule of thumb, for both children and adults, is to eat a variety of vegetables, fruits, whole grains, and beans, and add a multivitamin or other source of vitamin B12, such as enriched nondairy milk.

Children who eat vegan on a full-time basis gain real advantages. They are largely protected from the problems their meat-eating friends are likely to encounter: obesity, heart disease, diabetes, and certain cancers. And they are likely to live years longer. Researchers have learned that children following plant-based diets reach the same height as nonvegetarian children. And they tend to be slightly leaner and they are less likely to be overweight as adults.

If all this sounds challenging, keep in mind that when health authorities first recommended smokefree environments for children, a lot of people were slow to take the advice. The same was true for bicycle helmets and athletic safety gear. But the data is now in, and we now know that taking a bit of extra care of our children—and that means a healthy diet, first and foremost—can really pay off.

Healthy wishes,

Neal D. Barnard, M.D.
Founder and President of Physicians Committee
for Responsible Medicine

Vegan Pantry

So, you want to start cooking incredibly delicious vegan meals but need help stocking your pantry? Here's a handy guide to some ingredients and essentials that you may want to get familiar with before you start cooking.

FATS AND OILS

Canola oil

Canola oil is my go-to cooking oil. It is low in saturated fat yet high in healthful omega-3 fatty acids. It is very mild tasting and has a high smoke point. All of these qualities make it an excellent choice for cooking and baking, and for frying at high temperatures. Other mild oils include vegetable, safflower, and grapeseed oil, all of which can be used in place of canola oil.

Coconut oil

Coconut oil, which is pressed from *copra* (dried coconut meat), is one of the few saturated fats that does not come from an animal and is actually very healthful. It is high in lauric acid, which has many antiviral, antibacterial, and antioxidant properties that fight illnesses such as heart disease, diabetes, cancer, and HIV. It is also cholesterol and trans-fat free. Because coconut oil is quite heat stable, it is perfect to use for high-heat cooking or frying. It can keep on your pantry shelf for up to two years.

Coconut oil is solid at room temperature, which makes it great for baking. Unrefined coconut oil has a coconut flavor; refined coconut oil does not. Feel free to substitute refined coconut oil for vegan margarine or vegetable shortening in equal proportions in my recipes. It works especially well as a substitute in my frostings and pastry crusts.

Vegan margarine

Vegan margarine is a terrific substitute for butter in vegan cooking and baking. My favorite brand of vegan margarine is Earth Balance. It's made from a blend of oils and comes in soy-free varieties. It is all natural, nonhydrogenated, and trans-fat free. You can buy it at your local grocery store or natural foods market.

Nonhydrogenated vegetable shortening

Shortening is a solidified blend of oils that is great for making creamy frostings and flaky piecrusts. To make sure you are choosing the most healthful option, look for packaging that says "nonhydrogenated." Spectrum Organics and Earth Balance are excellent brands.

Olive oil

Olive oil is rich in antioxidants and vitamin E, is a great source of heart-healthful monounsaturated fat, and helps to lower cholesterol. Olive oil is a good choice for medium-heat cooking, such as sautéing and browning. It is also great in salad dressings and sauces, and for drizzling on finished dishes.

Sesame oil

There are two types of sesame oils. One is light in color and flavor and adds a slightly nutty taste to salad dressings and sautés. It has a high smoke point and can be used for frying. The second is toasted sesame oil, which is darker in color, richer in flavor, and often used in Asian dishes. It has a lower smoke point, so it is best used in stir-frying and for seasoning a finished dish.

Capers

Capers are the pickled buds of the caper bush. They are pickled in salt or a vinegar brine and are quite pungent. Capers are delicious with vegetables and in salads. They can be found in jars in the pickle and olive section of most grocery stores.

Chili-garlic sauce

This spicy Asian condiment can be found in the Asian section of any grocery store. If you don't have it on hand, you can spice up your dish with crushed red pepper or spicy chili sauce instead.

Chocolate chips

I use semisweet chocolate chips in many of my dessert recipes. They can be used whole or melted. Many brands, such as Ghiradelli or Guittard, make semisweet chocolate chips that are dairy free. You can also buy chocolate chips that are labeled "dairy-free" or "vegan" at your local natural foods market.

Hoisin sauce

Hoisin (pronounced HOY-sin) sauce is a thick, concentrated Asian condiment made from soybeans that has a sweet, salty, and spicy flavor. It can be found in the Asian section in any grocery store.

Gluten-free hoisin sauce is also available and can be found at your local natural foods market. Premier Japan, a popular brand, makes organic gluten-free hoisin sauce.

Instant espresso powder

Espresso powder is a very dark and strong instant coffee. I use it in many of my dessert recipes for flavoring. I use Medaglia D'Oro brand, which can be found in the coffee aisle at any grocery store or purchased online. If you cannot find espresso powder, you can use finely ground instant coffee measure for measure. You can also use decaffeinated instant espresso or coffee, if desired.

Mirin

Mirin is similar to sake but with a lower alcohol content. It is a sweet golden rice wine that is used to flavor Japanese glazes and sauces. The flavor is quite strong, so use it sparingly.

Miso paste

Miso is a fermented soybean paste, rich in protein and B vitamins, with amazing healing and immune-boosting qualities. There are many different varieties of miso. I prefer to use a mellow white or yellow miso because they are sweet and mild in flavor. Miso paste is used in soups, sauces, marinades, and dips.

Nutritional yeast flakes

Not to be confused with brewer's yeast, nutritional yeast has a roasted, nutty, cheese-like flavor. It is a good source of amino acids and B vitamins, and most brands are naturally gluten-free. Nutritional yeast is what gives my Best-Ever Baked Macaroni and Cheese (page 127) its yellow color and cheesy flavor. You can find nutritional yeast flakes in the bulk aisle in most natural foods markets, or in the Whole Body (supplements/wellness) section of Whole Foods Market. Bob's Red Mill, KAL, and Bragg are excellent brands that can also be purchased online.

Salt

Salt brings out and brightens the flavors of food. I like to cook with sea salt, which is unrefined, unbleached, and rich in health-supportive trace minerals. The taste is also far superior to white table salt. *Fleur de sel* is a moist, hand-harvested sea salt from France that is best used as a finishing salt, as in my Sea Salt Toffee Bars (page 233).

Soy sauce

Soy sauce adds flavor, saltiness, and color to many Asian-inspired dishes. Shoyu and tamari are two variations. Shoyu is a natural soy sauce made from fermented soybeans and grains; tamari is wheat-free.

For Soy-Free Soy Sauce, try my homemade recipe on page 257.

Tahini

Tahini is a thick paste made from ground sesame seeds; it is a common ingredient in Middle Eastern cooking.

FLOURS

Wheat flour

There are a variety of flours to cook and bake with. Many of my recipes call for unbleached all-purpose flour, which is also known as regular white flour and yields a light and tender product. Whole-wheat pastry flour is an unrefined alternative to all-purpose flour. If you prefer, you can use half whole-wheat pastry flour and half unbleached all-purpose flour in my recipes.

Cornmeal

Cornmeal is a flour made by grinding dried corn kernels. The two most common types of cornmeal are yellow and white, with yellow being a little bit sweeter. I use yellow cornmeal in many of my recipes.

Garbanzo flour

Garbanzo flour is made from dried garbanzo beans (chickpeas) and is rich in protein. It is gluten-free and can be substituted for wheat flour in many of my savory recipes.

Gluten-free flour (page 11)

GRAINS

A grain is a small hard seed that comes in many different varieties. The most common grains are wheat, rice, rye, barley, and corn. Quinoa is considered a supergrain. It is a complete protein because it contains all eight essential amino acids. For information about cooking grains, see page 251 in the Basics Chapter.

Legumes

The legume family includes beans, lentils, peas, and peanuts. They are a good source of protein and fiber. For information about cooking dried beans, see page 251 in the Basics Chapter.

Tempeh

Tempeh (pronounced TEM-pay) is a fermented soy product that is extremely high in protein and fiber. It originates from Indonesia and has a nutty texture and mild flavor. Don't be alarmed if you see black spots on the tempeh. That is a completely normal sign of the fermentation process. Opened packages of tempeh will keep for up to ten days in the refrigerator and up to three months in the freezer. Tempeh can be crumbled, sliced, diced, or marinated, and used as a meat substitute. It can be found in the refrigerated section of your local natural foods market next to the tofu.

Seitan

Seitan (pronounced SAY-tan) is made from the protein in wheat flour, gluten. It is chewy, hearty, and soaks up savory sauces very well. It is made from a simple process of mixing wheat flour and water (see Homemade Seitan, on page 252). You can also buy packaged seitan at your local natural foods market.

Tofu

Commonly used in vegetarian cooking, tofu is high in protein and iron and very low in calories and fat. It is made from soybeans and will take on the flavor of any dressing, marinade, or sauce, making it a versatile meat substitute. There are two kinds of tofu that I like to cook with: soft and extra-firm. Soft (or silken) tofu is great for blending into salad dressings or dips. Extra-firm tofu can be crumbled, baked, and stir-fried. Any leftover tofu can be kept in a container, covered in fresh water, for up to five days, in the refrigerator. Change the water every two days. Tofu freezes well. When thawed, the texture will be firm and chewy, which makes it perfect for savory dishes.

Mushrooms

Mushrooms are the only vegetable that I am addressing in the pantry because they have a juicy and meaty texture, making them a fabulous choice in vegan cooking. They are rich in antioxidants, protein, and fiber. Mushrooms are also a great source of minerals, such as selenium, that fight heart disease and cancer. Choose mushrooms that are firm and dry, and wipe them clean with a damp towel. Trim the stem ends of all mushrooms before using. Remember to discard the stems of shiitake mushrooms because they are tough and difficult to digest. The mushrooms I use most frequently are: crimini, portobello, baby bella, shiitake, oyster, and porcini.

NONDAIRY MILK

There are many varieties of nondairy milk including soy, almond, rice, and coconut. They are healthful low-fat alternatives for anyone who wants to avoid dairy. Nondairy milks are often enriched with vitamins, and are cholesterol and lactose free. They come in plain, unsweetened, chocolate, and vanilla flavors. You can purchase many nondairy milks in refrigerated cartons or aseptic containers, which do not have to be refrigerated and are perfect for lunch boxes and traveling.

Soy milk

Soy milk is made from soybeans and water and has almost as much protein as cow's milk but is cholesterol free and low in saturated fat.

Almond milk

Almond milk is made from pulverized almonds and water. The almond flavor is very subtle. Almond milk is thick and has added vitamins such as calcium and vitamin D. It has no saturated fat, is cholesterol free, and very low in calories.

Rice milk

Rice milk is a great alternative for those who are allergic to nuts or soy. Milled rice is mixed with water, creating a thinner milk, and is enriched with vitamins. It is low in sodium, has no saturated fat and no cholesterol.

Coconut milk

Coconut milk is thick and creamy, making it a great nondairy milk to use in Asian sauces, curries, and desserts. The fat in coconut milk is a healthful good fat, does not contribute to heart disease, and is beneficial to the cardiovascular system.

You can buy coconut milk canned or in cartons in the refrigerated section of your grocery store. I prefer to use canned coconut milk, which is slightly thicker. With the exception of my Coconut Whipped Cream recipe (page 239), you can substitute lite canned coconut milk, which is lower in fat.

PASTA

Brown Rice noodles

Brown rice noodles are made from brown rice and water. They have a slightly softer texture than wheat noodles and are gluten-free. They take longer to cook than wheat noodles.

Soba noodles

Soba is Japanese for buckwheat. Soba noodles are made from buckwheat and wheat flours.

Udon noodles

Udon noodles are Japanese noodles made from wheat flour. They are thick and wide, with a soft chewy texture. Udon noodles are usually used in soup.

PASTRY DOUGHS

Phyllo dough

Phyllo, also spelled "filo," is a very thin pastry dough popular in Mediterranean and Middle Eastern cooking. Phyllo dough can be found at your local grocery store in the freezer section near the piecrusts. See my tip for working with phyllo dough on page 37.

Puff pastry

Puff pastry is a layered dough that makes a tender flaky pastry crust. It can be bought in sheets at your local grocery store in the freezer section near the piecrusts. You can find some brands of puff pastry that are dairy-free and nonhydrogenated. Check the label to be sure.

SWEETENERS

Sugar

When choosing granulated or powdered sugar to bake with, I always look for words like organic, fair trade, and vegan on the package because some refined sugars are processed using animal bone char. Wholesome Sweeteners, Florida Crystals, and

Whole Foods 365 brand are all good quality brands that make specifically vegan sugars.

Agave

Agave nectar is a natural, unrefined liquid sweetener that is extracted from the leaves of the Mexican agave plant. Agave is sweeter than sugar, and has a lower glycemic index, too. I prefer to use light agave because of its mild flavor and clear color, but you can also buy it in darker varieties.

Maple syrup

Maple syrup is a natural unrefined liquid sweetener that is good for more than just pouring over pancakes. It has a distinct taste that can enhance and sweeten the flavor of many savory dishes and baked goods.

THICKENERS

Xanthan gum

Xanthan gum is a fine powder that is used for thickening, stabilizing, and emulsifying. I use xanthan gum when making ice cream from scratch because it adds thickness. Xanthan gum is also a key ingredient in gluten-free baking. Whenever you use Bob's Red Mill Gluten-Free All-Purpose Flour, it is best to add xanthan gum as directed on the back of the flour package. You can buy xanthan gum from most natural food markets or online at BobsRedMill.com.

Cornstarch and arrowroot

Cornstarch is a fine powder made from corn kernels. Arrowroot is a fine powder prepared from the rootstalks of a tropical tuber. Both cornstarch and arrowroot are used as thickeners in sauces, gravies, and custards. Arrowroot is a great corn-free alternative to cornstarch; they can be used interchangeably.

VINEGAR

Vinegar adds tanginess and flavor to food. Vinegar is also used frequently in vegan baking to replace eggs. When combined with baking soda, vinegar helps baked goods bind together and rise. The types of vinegar that I use most often are white, apple cider, balsamic, malt, and rice.

Vitamix

Vitamix is considered the Rolls Royce of blenders, perfect for blending nuts to an ultrasmooth cream and whipping up a smoothie in seconds! It is a high-speed, heavy-duty, powerful machine, available in restaurant supply stores, warehouse stores, and online.

Food processor

A food processor is the workhorse of the kitchen. The processor can be used to chop, grind, grate, cut, slice, puree, and blend foods. I recommend getting at least an eleven-cup capacity food processor, although you can always work with a smaller one in batches.

Parchment paper

Parchment paper is nonstick. It is available in both rolls and sheets. Use it on baking sheets to prevent baked goods from sticking to the pan. Parchment paper is preferred over wax paper because wax paper is not always oven safe.

Silpat

Silpat is a fiberglass and silicone nonstick baking mat that never needs greasing and can be used over and over again. It is available in various sizes and is easy to clean. If preferred, it can be used in place of parchment paper for baking.

Stand or hand mixer

Electric stand mixers are useful for kneading doughs, mixing batters, and beating frostings. If you do not have the kitchen space for a stand mixer, a hand-held electric mixer will work too.

Ice cream maker

Ice cream makers come in a range of shapes, sizes, and prices. You do not need to buy an expensive industrial ice cream maker to make my ice cream recipes.

Gluten-Free and Soy-Free Cooking

Most of the recipes in this book can be made gluten-free and soy-free by using the substitutions listed here. If you are preparing a recipe for yourself or someone else with a food allergy, check all ingredient labels carefully to make sure that they are allergen-free. It is up to the consumer to avoid ingredients that contain allergens, allergen derivatives, or have been exposed to cross-contamination.

GLUTEN-FREE SUBSTITUTES

Flour

Bob's Red Mill Gluten-Free All-Purpose Baking Flour is an excellent product that can be used in many of my sweet and savory recipes calling for flour. It is made from a blend of garbanzo flour and potato starch, and can be found at your local grocery store or ordered online at BobsRedMill.com. There are many brands of gluten-free flour, but I get the best results with Bob's Red Mill. When substituting gluten-free flour in a recipe, make sure that the other ingredients you are using in the recipe are gluten-free as well, such as pasta, bread products, and seasonings.

Note that gluten-free flour can be used in almost all of my dessert recipes with excellent results, but it is very important to add xanthan gum (page 9) as directed in the recipe. Also, baking time may vary when using gluten-free flour.

Pasta

Brown rice pasta is a delicious alternative to wheat pasta. You can use it in every single one of my pasta recipes. Brown rice pasta takes longer to cook, so be sure to boil it until it is tender with a soft bite. You can also use quinoa pasta, which has a beautiful golden color.

Bread

Gluten-free bread, often made from rice, flax, and almond flour can be purchased at your local natural foods market and substituted in all recipes calling for bread. It is usually found in the freezer section of the grocery store.

Soy Sauce

Gluten-free tamari can be found at your local natural foods market and used in place of soy sauce. San-J is a popular brand that carries organic gluten-free soy sauce.

Seitan

For gluten-free cooking, avoid seitan, which is made from pure wheat gluten. Instead, substitute extra-firm tofu or tempeh.

Hoisin Sauce

Gluten-free hoisin sauce can be found at your local natural foods market. Premier Japan is a popular brand that carries organic gluten-free hoisin sauce.

Bread crumbs

Use store-bought gluten-free bread crumbs or make your own by toasting gluten-free bread and pulsing it in a food processor until it becomes fine crumbs.

SOY-FREE SUBSTITUTES

Tofu and tempeh

For soy-free cooking, avoid tofu or tempeh. In recipes that use pieces of tofu or tempeh, such as Pineapple Not-So-Fried Rice (page 185) or Tempeh Piccata (page 191), use seitan instead. In recipes that use crumbled or ground tempeh, such as Double Double Drive-Thru Burgers (page 103) or Sweet-and-Sour Party Meatballs (page 33), substitute 1 cup cooked brown rice per 8 ounces tempeh.

Soy sauce

My recipe for Soy-Free Soy Sauce (page 257) can be used in place of soy sauce.

Margarine

Earth Balance is the leading brand of vegan margarine; it is also available in a soy-free version.

Small Bites

Artichoke-Walnut Pesto Crostini

SERVES 6 TO 8

Sometimes I wonder why I even bother with dinner after I've served these crostini as an appetizer. They are so irresistible that my friends enthusiastically shovel them down like a main course. Made with walnuts, which are rich in omega 3s, and lightened with a splash of lemon, this is a healthful alternative to traditional pesto and much more flavorful. Simply slather the pesto on olive-oil-drizzled crostini (Italian for "little toasts") for this perfect appetizer that takes all of ten minutes to make.

Make-Ahead Tip

The pesto can be made in advance and kept frozen for up to 1 month or refrigerated for 2 to 3 days. Thaw and mix well before serving.

14 ounces canned, marinated, or frozen artichoke hearts, drained

1 cup packed fresh Italian parsley

¾ cup walnuts, toasted

3 cloves garlic

2 tablespoons lemon juice

¾ teaspoon sea salt

¾ teaspoon freshly ground black pepper

¼ cup olive oil, plus extra for drizzling

¼ cup water

1 baguette, cut into ½-inch slices on the diagonal

Preheat the oven to 425 degrees.

In a food processor, pulse artichoke hearts, parsley, walnuts, garlic, lemon juice, salt, pepper, ¼ cup oil, and water until combined.

Place bread slices on a large baking tray and drizzle lightly with oil. Bake 5 to 8 minutes, or until lightly browned.

Spread pesto on warm or cooled crostini and transfer to a serving platter.

Avocado-Shiitake Sushi

SERVES 4 TO 6

Who needs raw fish when you've got creamy avocado and succulent shiitake mushrooms coated in sweet teriyaki sauce? This is the ultimate sushi combo and I request it at every Japanese restaurant I go to, even when it's not on the menu. I know the fast and fancy action behind a sushi bar can look pretty intimidating, but my recipe is extremely easy and beginner friendly. You can also use this recipe to make tempura rolls by substituting sweet potato or asparagus Vegetable Tempura (page 91) for the shiitake mushrooms. Ready, set, roll!

3 cups cooked short-grain brown or white rice

2 tablespoons canola oil

6 ounces shiitake mushrooms, stemmed and thinly sliced

1 cup teriyaki sauce, purchased or prepared following recipe on page 83

⅓ cup brown or white rice vinegar

2 tablespoons agave

1½ teaspoons sea salt

4 sheets toasted nori

1 avocado, pitted, peeled, and thinly sliced, see Tip (page 32)

Soy sauce for dipping, optional

Wasabi, optional

Cook rice according to package directions. While rice is cooking, prepare other ingredients.

In a large skillet, heat oil over medium-high heat, and sauté mushrooms until soft and lightly browned. Add teriyaki sauce and cook until heated through. Remove mushrooms from skillet with a slotted spoon and reserve sauce.

Whisk together vinegar, agave, and salt in a small bowl. Transfer warm cooked rice to a large baking sheet. Slowly drizzle the vinegar mixture onto the rice, while gently folding the rice with a large spoon or spatula. Do not stir the rice or it will get mushy. Cover with a damp towel and let cool to room temperature.

To assemble sushi: Lay a sheet of nori, shiny side down, in front of you on a flat surface or bamboo sushi mat. With wet fingertips, press ¾ cup cooled rice onto the nori, leaving a 1-inch border on the top and bottom and a ½-inch border on the two sides. On top of the rice, layer one quarter of the teriyaki mushrooms and 2 to 3 slices of avocado, parallel to your body, 2 inches from the edge of nori that is closest to you. Roll the nori away from you tightly, like you are rolling a yoga mat or sleeping bag. Seal the roll with a little water. Using a sharp knife, cut ½ inch off each edge of the nori roll to make clean edges. Slice the nori roll into ¾-inch pieces.

Serve sushi with reserved teriyaki sauce or soy sauce and wasabi.

Balsamic Bruschetta

SERVES 6 TO 8

Warm, crusty baguette topped with fresh tomatoes, basil, and garlic is a colorful way to start any dinner party. The syrupy Balsamic Reduction adds an extra sweet kick, creating an explosion of flavors. Ka-boom!

BALSAMIC REDUCTION

1 cup balsamic vinegar

1 tablespoon maple syrup

BRUSCHETTA

6 Roma plum tomatoes, diced
½ cup chopped fresh basil
3 cloves garlic, minced
1 tablespoon balsamic vinegar
1 tablespoon olive oil, plus extra for drizzling

¼ teaspoon sea salt
¼ teaspoon freshly ground black pepper
1 baguette, cut into ½-inch slices on the diagonal

To make the Balsamic Reduction: In a small saucepan, cook vinegar over medium-low heat until it comes to a boil. Reduce heat and simmer, uncovered, for 20 minutes, or until it reduces to a thick syrupy consistency. Remove from heat and stir in the maple syrup.

To make the Bruschetta: Preheat the oven to 425 degrees.

In a large bowl, toss tomatoes, basil, garlic, vinegar, 1 tablespoon oil, salt, and pepper. Set aside while flavors come together.

Place bread slices on a large baking tray and drizzle lightly with olive oil. Bake 5 to 8 minutes, or until lightly browned on top.

Place slices on a platter, top each slice with the tomato mixture, and drizzle the Balsamic Reduction lightly on top.

Black Bean Baby Cakes with Pineapple Salsa

MAKES 16 2-INCH PATTIES

I posted a recipe for Black Bean Sliders on my blog awhile back, and the response was huge. *One reader even wrote that her family held an arm-wrestling contest to determine who got the last slider. The things we do for food! For this recipe, I decided to ditch the bun and get to the good stuff: a savory spiced black bean cake topped with a sweet and tangy tropical salsa. Don't forget to save a secret stash for yourself!*

Make-Ahead Tip

Uncooked Black Bean Baby Cakes can be frozen for up to 1 month or refrigerated for 3 to 4 days before pan-frying. The Pineapple Salsa can be made in advance and kept refrigerated for 3 to 4 days.

BLACK BEAN BABY CAKES

4 tablespoons olive oil, divided

1 onion, finely chopped

1 15-ounce can black beans, rinsed and drained

1 small carrot, peeled and finely diced or shredded (about ½ cup)

½ cup cornmeal

½ cup bread crumbs

1 tablespoon chili powder

1 teaspoon sea salt

½ cup chopped fresh cilantro

¼ cup water

PINEAPPLE SALSA

1 cup diced pineapple

¼ cup finely chopped fresh cilantro

2 tablespoons finely chopped red onion

1 tablespoon agave, optional, for extra sweetness

To make the Black Bean Baby Cakes: In a large nonstick skillet, heat 2 tablespoons oil over medium heat. Add onions and let cook until tender and slightly caramelized, about 20 minutes. Transfer onions to a large bowl. Reserve skillet for later use.

Add beans, carrots, cornmeal, bread crumbs, chili powder, salt, cilantro, and water to the bowl of onions. Use a large spoon or your hands to mash it all together. If the mixture is too dry to hold together, add water, 1 tablespoon at a time.

Using your hands, form the bean mixture into patties, about 2 inches in diameter. In the reserved nonstick skillet, heat remaining 2 tablespoons oil over medium-high heat, and pan-fry patties about 3 minutes on each side, until lightly browned and crisp. Add more oil to the skillet as needed. Drain patties on paper towels.

To make the Pineapple Salsa: Combine all ingredients.

Arrange Black Bean Baby Cakes on a platter, top each cake with a spoonful of Pineapple Salsa, and serve.

Crispy Potato-Leek Patties with Lemon-Dill Dip

MAKES 32 BITE-SIZED PATTIES

With crispy edges and mashed potato-leek centers, these patties go perfectly with a dollop of cool and refreshing Lemon-Dill Dip. They can be served as an appetizer or paired with any entrée as a delicious alternative to mashed potatoes.

Leeks, like onions and garlic, are in the allium family. They look like enormous scallions but have a milder flavor.

CRISPY POTATO-LEEK PATTIES

2 russet potatoes, peeled and cut into 1-inch pieces

1 leek, see Tip

4 tablespoons olive oil, divided

Sea salt

Freshly ground black pepper

¼ cup all-purpose flour, or gluten-free all-purpose flour

LEMON-DILL DIP

12 ounces soft tofu

1 clove garlic

2 tablespoons lemon juice

2 tablespoons chopped fresh dill

½ teaspoon yellow or Dijon mustard

½ teaspoon sea salt

To make the Potato-Leek Patties: Place potatoes in a medium saucepan and fill it with enough water to cover the potatoes. Heavily salt the water and bring to a boil. Let the potatoes boil until fork tender. In the meantime, prepare leek.

Heat 2 tablespoons oil in a large nonstick skillet over medium-high heat, and sauté leeks until soft and lightly browned. Season with salt and pepper, and transfer to a large bowl. Reserve skillet for later use.

When potatoes are ready, drain and mash them. Add mashed potatoes and flour to the bowl of leeks, and season generously with salt and pepper. Mix well. Using 1 tablespoon of potato mixture at a time, form into small patties, about ½-inch thick.

Heat remaining 2 tablespoons oil in the reserved nonstick skillet over medium-high heat, and pan-fry patties in batches, adding more oil as needed. When the bottom of each patty is browned and crisp, flip, and let it cook on the other side. Remove from pan and drain on paper towels.

To make the Lemon-Dill Dip: In a blender, combine tofu, garlic, lemon juice, dill, mustard, and salt. Blend until smooth. Adjust seasoning to taste.

To serve: Arrange Crispy Potato-Leek Patties on a serving platter and top each one with a dollop of Lemon-Dill Dip.

. . . .

Chloe's Tip: Cleaning Leeks

Leeks can be very sandy, so they need to be cleaned well before using. First, rinse them and cut off the dark green leaves and the root, leaving the white and light green parts. Cut the remaining stalk in half, lengthwise. Lay the leek halves on your cutting surface with the flat sides down, and slice thinly into half-rounds. Place the leeks in a large bowl and add enough cold water to cover them. Let the leeks soak, swishing the water a few times to loosen the sand. The sand will sink to the bottom of the bowl. Scoop the leeks out of the water with your hands or a strainer onto a towel and dry them. Do not pour the leeks and water into a colander or strainer because you will just be transferring the sand with the leeks.

. . . .

Garlic Knots

I make these restaurant-style knots of garlicky goodness out of pizza dough. They are glistening and crusty on the outside with a warm, doughy center. I once set a large tray of these on the dinner table in front of my brother Andy, expecting him to take one and pass it down; let's just say the tray didn't make it to anybody else. I couldn't blame him because these two-bite knots are finger-lickin' good!

Flour, for rolling
1 to 1½ pounds pizza dough, purchased or prepared following recipe on page 250
4 to 5 cloves garlic, minced
½ cup olive oil, plus more for brushing

¼ cup finely chopped fresh Italian parsley
¼ teaspoon sea salt
¼ teaspoon freshly ground black pepper

Preheat the oven to 375 degrees. Brush 2 large baking sheets with oil.

On a well-floured surface, roll out the pizza dough into two 12 x 10-inch rectangles. Working with one rectangle at a time, place the shorter side facing you and cut the dough in

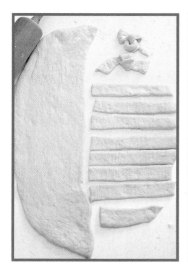

(continued on next page)

half lengthwise. Cut each half, crosswise, into about ten 1-inch wide strips. Loosely tie each strip of dough into a knot, stretching carefully as needed. Place 20 knots, about 1 inch apart, on each prepared baking sheet and lightly brush the tops with oil. Bake for 20 to 25 minutes until golden brown on top. Let cool for a few minutes.

Combine garlic, oil, parsley, salt, and pepper in a large bowl. Add warm knots to the bowl and toss until each knot is coated. Remove knots from the oil and serve warm.

Garlic White Bean Dip

MAKES ABOUT 1¼ CUPS

This better-than-hummus dip is creamy garlicky good. It comes together in seconds and can be prepared the day before.

1 15-ounce can cannellini or other white
    beans, rinsed and drained
¼ cup olive oil
2 tablespoons water
1 tablespoon lemon juice

2 cloves garlic
½ teaspoon dried thyme
1 teaspoon sea salt
½ teaspoon freshly ground black
    pepper

Blend all ingredients in a food processor until smooth. Serve with sliced baguette, pita bread wedges, chips, crackers, or raw veggies.

Kalamata Olive Tapenade

MAKES ABOUT 1 CUP

This tapenade is so simple and tastes much better than store-bought olive spread. You can buy Kalamata olives bottled, canned, or at a fresh olive bar. Either way, this is an easy way to serve up a delicious Mediterranean appetizer that is loaded with vitamin E.

1 cup pitted Kalamata olives
1 tablespoon drained capers
2 cloves garlic

2 teaspoons lemon juice
¼ teaspoon freshly ground black
    pepper

Pulse all ingredients in a food processor until spreadable. Serve in a small bowl with crackers or a sliced baguette.

Jalapeño Cornbread Poppers with Whipped Maple Butter

MAKES 24 BITE-SIZED POPPERS

Once you pop, the fun won't stop! These poppers are crispy on the outside, fluffy on the inside, and are served with sweet maple butter to soothe the hot jalapeño bite. Grab 'em while you can; if your family's anything like mine, these poppers will vanish in a flash.

WHIPPED MAPLE BUTTER

1 cup vegan margarine, at room temperature

¼ cup maple syrup

JALAPEÑO CORNBREAD POPPERS

1 cup cornmeal

¾ cup all-purpose flour

1 teaspoon salt

4 teaspoons baking powder

1 tablespoon sugar

⅔ cup soy, almond, or rice milk

½ jalapeño, seeded and finely chopped

½ cup corn kernels, fresh or frozen

Canola oil, for frying

To make the Whipped Maple Butter: In a mixing bowl, using a whisk or electric mixer, whip margarine with maple syrup until light and fluffy. Refrigerate until serving.

To make the Jalapeño Cornbread Poppers: In a medium bowl, whisk together cornmeal, flour, salt, baking powder, and sugar. Mix in nondairy milk, jalapeño, and corn with a large spoon until combined. Using the palms of your hands, form into 1-inch balls. Set aside.

Fill a deep-sided heavy skillet or deep fryer with about 2 inches of oil. Heat to 350 degrees, or until a drop of batter sizzles when added. Fry the poppers in batches. Oil should sizzle around the poppers. Let each popper fry for about 1 to 2 minutes, turning halfway through, until crispy and lightly browned on the outside. Drain on paper towels. Serve immediately with the Whipped Maple Butter and keep 'em coming!

Mini Potato Skins Stuffed with Avocado Salsa

SERVES 10

Holy vegan guacamole! This is my amazing California take on double-stuffed potatoes. Crispy scooped-out mini potato skins filled with chunky avocado salsa—need I say more?

MINI POTATO SKINS
....

10 small (2-inch diameter) new potatoes, red or white

2 tablespoons olive oil

½ teaspoon sea salt

¼ teaspoon freshly ground black pepper

AVOCADO SALSA
....

3 avocados, pitted, peeled, and diced, see Tip (page 32)

2 tablespoons lemon or lime juice

¼ cup salsa fresca (see note, page 32)

½ teaspoon sea salt

½ teaspoon ground cumin

Freshly ground black pepper

To make the Mini Potato Skins: Preheat the oven to 375 degrees.

In a large bowl, toss potatoes with oil, salt, and pepper. Spread potatoes on a large baking sheet, and bake for 45 minutes, or until tender. Remove from oven, and let potatoes rest until they are cool to the touch. Cut potatoes in half and scoop out the centers with a spoon or melon baller. Save the insides for another use, like mashed potatoes.

Turn the oven to 400 degrees. Place the scooped out potato skins cut side up on a large baking sheet and bake for an additional 15 minutes until the edges are crisp.

To make the Avocado Salsa: In a medium bowl, using a large spoon, gently mix avocado, lemon juice, salsa fresca, salt, cumin, and a few grinds of pepper. Adjust seasoning to taste.

To serve: Stuff each potato skin with a spoonful of Avocado Salsa. Plate and serve.

(continued on next page)

Note: Make salsa fresca by combining 1 seeded and diced medium tomato, 1 tablespoon finely chopped red onion, and 1 tablespoon finely chopped fresh cilantro.

. . . .

Chloe's Tip: Cutting Avocados

With a long sharp knife, cut the avocado lengthwise around the pit. Twist the halves to separate, exposing the pit. Hit the pit with the blade of the knife with just enough force to wedge the knife into the pit. Twist the knife; the pit should come right out. Use a large spoon to scoop the flesh out of each half in one piece. Place the avocado halves on a cutting board and cut as desired.

. . . .

Sweet-and-Sour Party Meatballs

MAKES 42 MEATBALLS

Get your party started with this retro classic that I've updated for the modern palate. When I was a Girl Scout in Troop 50, all of us made hundreds of meatballs to complete our cooking badges. We had so much fun shaping them while the moms fried them up. This memory inspired me to make a vegan version for this book. These saucy Sweet-and-Sour Party Meatballs are packed with protein and fiber, but are still kid-approved delicious!

Make-Ahead Tip

The meatball mixture can be made in advance, shaped into balls, and kept frozen for up to 1 month or refrigerated for 3 to 4 days until ready to cook. The Sweet-and-Sour Sauce can be made in advance and kept refrigerated for 3 to 4 days.

1 8-ounce package tempeh, or 1 cup cooked brown rice	½ cup all-purpose flour, or gluten-free all-purpose flour
2 tablespoons olive oil	1 teaspoon dried basil
1 onion, finely chopped	1 teaspoon sea salt
2 cloves garlic, minced	1 teaspoon freshly ground black pepper
1 15-ounce can lentils, rinsed and drained	2 tablespoons canola oil
1 cup walnuts, toasted	Sweet-and-Sour Sauce (page 256)

Fill a large pot with enough water to reach the bottom of a steamer basket. Using a knife or your hands, break tempeh into 4 pieces and place in the basket. Cover and steam for 20 minutes. Check the pot occasionally and add more water if necessary. Steaming the tempeh will remove its bitterness.

In the meantime, heat olive oil in a large nonstick skillet over medium-high heat, and sauté onions until soft and lightly browned. Add garlic and cook a few more minutes. Transfer to a food processor. Reserve skillet for later use.

Add steamed tempeh, lentils, walnuts, flour, basil, salt, and pepper to the onions in the food processor. Pulse until the walnut pieces are very fine and the mixture comes together. If

(continued on page 35)

Sweet-and-Sour Party Meatballs (*cont.*)

necessary, transfer the mixture to a large bowl and mix with your hands. Adjust seasoning to taste. With the palms of your hands, form the mixture into 1-inch balls.

Heat canola oil in reserved nonstick skillet over medium-high heat, and pan-fry meatballs in batches, adding more oil as needed. Rotate the meatballs with a wooden spoon so that they brown on all sides. Remove meatballs from the pan using 2 forks or a slotted spoon and drain on paper towels. Transfer meatballs to a serving platter and spoon Sweet-and-Sour Sauce on top.

Phyllo Mushroom Turnovers

MAKES 24 2-INCH TURNOVERS

Phyllo turnovers are popular party appetizers that typically rely on lots of cheese and butter for flavor. Not these! My low-fat recipe is light and elegant, made with savory herb- and wine-infused mushrooms. These flaky hot pastry pockets are also a cinch to assemble and can be made ahead and frozen.

Make-Ahead Tip

Freeze the unbaked turnovers on a baking sheet for 30 minutes to 1 hour until frozen. Store the frozen turnovers in the freezer in a sealed container or bag. When ready to bake, do not thaw. Remove turnovers from freezer and bake at 350 degrees for about 20 minutes, until lightly golden on top.

2 tablespoons olive oil, plus extra for brushing

8 ounces crimini mushrooms, trimmed and sliced

3 shallots, finely chopped

¼ teaspoon sea salt

¼ teaspoon freshly ground black pepper

¼ cup white wine

1 teaspoon chopped fresh thyme leaves

1 tablespoon chopped fresh Italian parsley

6 sheets phyllo dough, thawed according to package directions

To make the filling: In a medium skillet, heat oil over medium-high heat and sauté mushrooms, shallots, salt, and pepper, until mushrooms and shallots are soft and lightly browned. Add wine and let cook until it bubbles away. Turn off the heat, and add the thyme and parsley. Adjust seasoning to taste and let cool slightly. Transfer mushroom mixture to a food processor and pulse until mushrooms are roughly the size of small peas. Set aside.

To assemble and bake the turnovers: Preheat the oven to 375 degrees.

On a flat surface, layer 2 sheets phyllo dough and brush the top layer with oil. Using a sharp knife or pizza cutter, cut the phyllo dough, widthwise, into 8 equal short strips. Working with one strip at a time, fold up about ½ inch of the phyllo at one end, making a reinforcement for the filling. Place 2 teaspoons filling on the flap. Fold the corner to form a triangle over the filling. Continue folding the triangle, like a flag, and tuck the end edge under. Place on a baking sheet and lightly brush with oil. Make the remaining seven turnovers. Repeat the procedure with the remaining sheets of phyllo. Bake for about 12 to 15 minutes, or until lightly golden on top.

. . . .

Chloe's Tip: About Phyllo Dough

Phyllo dough can be found at your local grocery store, in the freezer section near the piecrusts. Thaw frozen packages of phyllo dough according to package directions. After unwrapping a package of phyllo dough, cover the sheets that are not being used immediately with a slightly damp towel so that they do not dry out. Most important, don't sweat it if the phyllo sheets tear and wrinkle. Imperfections will not be noticeable on the finished product. This is part of making a rustic flaky pastry!

. . . .

Samosas with Cilantro-Tamarind Dipping Sauce

MAKES 36 SAMOSAS

I made these popular Indian appetizers bite-sized so that they are easier to eat with fingers. You can use any leftover Roasted Cauliflower Curry filling in my award-winning Mango Masala Panini (page 101).

Make-Ahead Tip

The Roasted Cauliflower Curry and Cilantro-Tamarind Dipping Sauce can be made in advance and refrigerated for 3 to 4 days.

SAMOSA DOUGH

1½ cups all-purpose flour, plus extra for rolling

¾ teaspoon sea salt

1 tablespoon canola oil

½ cup water

ROASTED CAULIFLOWER CURRY

½ head cauliflower, cut into florets

4 tablespoons olive oil, divided

Sea salt

Freshly ground black pepper

1 small russet potato, peeled and diced

½ onion, finely chopped

1½ teaspoons curry powder

¼ teaspoon ground ginger

⅛ teaspoon turmeric

1½ tablespoons brown or black mustard seeds

1 tablespoon lemon juice

¼ cup frozen peas

CILANTRO-TAMARIND DIPPING SAUCE

½ cup agave

¼ cup olive oil

1 tablespoon balsamic vinegar

½ teaspoon tamarind paste

1 cup fresh cilantro

2 scallions, trimmed and thinly sliced

1 teaspoon ground cumin

Canola oil, for frying

To make the Samosa Dough: In a medium bowl, whisk together flour and salt. Using a fork, stir in oil, creating a crumbly consistency. Slowly drizzle water into flour a little at a time, mixing continuously. Knead with your hands until a stiff dough has formed. Cover with plastic wrap and set aside for 30 minutes.

To make the Roasted Cauliflower Curry: Preheat oven to 400 degrees.

In a large bowl, toss cauliflower with 2 tablespoons olive oil and generously season with salt and pepper. Transfer cauliflower to a 9 x 13-inch pan and roast for 30 minutes, or until florets are fork tender. If cauliflower begins to burn, cover with foil. Remove from oven, let cool slightly, and pulse until finely chopped. Set aside.

In the meantime, place potatoes in a small saucepan and cover with salted water. Bring to a boil and let cook until fork tender. Drain and set aside.

In a medium skillet, heat remaining 2 tablespoons oil over medium heat and sauté onion with ½ teaspoon salt until soft and lightly browned. Add curry powder, ginger, turmeric, and mustard seeds, and cook for a few more minutes until fragrant. Transfer onion mixture to a large bowl and add roasted cauliflower, potatoes, and lemon juice. Mash together and stir in peas. Adjust seasoning to taste.

To make the Cilantro-Tamarind Dipping Sauce: In a food processor, pulse agave, oil, vinegar, tamarind paste, cilantro, scallions, and cumin until cilantro leaves are small green specks and all ingredients are incorporated.

To assemble and cook Samosas: On a lightly floured surface, roll out dough to ⅛-inch thick (about the thickness of a tortilla). Using a 4-inch cookie cutter or glass, cut out rounds. Cut each round in half. Spoon ½ to 1 teaspoon Roasted Cauliflower Curry onto the center of each half moon. Bring the corners together and press the edges together to seal. If necessary, moisten edges with water for a better seal.

Fill a large heavy-bottomed skillet with about ½ inch of oil. Heat oil over medium heat. Carefully place samosas in oil; do not crowd pan. Fry samosas until lightly golden brown on each side. Drain on paper towels. Serve with Cilantro-Tamarind Dipping Sauce.

Warm Spinach-Artichoke Dip

SERVES 8 TO 10

My whole life I've been a hold-the-mayo kind of girl. In third grade, when I found out that spinach artichoke dip is often made with mayo, I said goodbye to that creamy dip forever! Until, of course, I created this mayo-free, low-fat, vegan version that totally knocks my socks off. It's easy, delicious, and mayo-hater friendly!

2 tablespoons olive oil	2 tablespoons lemon juice
1 onion, roughly chopped	1 teaspoon dried basil
3 cloves garlic, minced	1½ teaspoons sea salt
½ teaspoon crushed red pepper, optional	½ teaspoon freshly ground black pepper
5 ounces baby spinach	14 ounces of canned, marinated, or frozen artichoke hearts, drained
1 14-ounce package soft tofu, drained	Bread or tortilla chips for serving
½ cup nutritional yeast flakes	

Preheat the oven to 350 degrees. Lightly grease a 1-quart baking dish.

In a large skillet, heat oil over medium-high heat and sauté onions until soft. Add garlic and red pepper and let cook a few more minutes. Reduce the heat to medium-low and add spinach. Let cook, stirring gently, until spinach is wilted.

In a food processor, blend tofu, nutritional yeast, lemon juice, basil, salt, and pepper until smooth. Add artichokes and spinach mixture, and pulse about 15 times. Transfer to the prepared baking dish.

Bake for 30 minutes, or until lightly browned on top. Let cool a few minutes, then serve with bread or tortilla chips.

Wontons with Apricot-Mustard Sauce

MAKES 14 DUMPLINGS

Ginger shiitake filling enveloped in a pan-fried noodle and dipped in sweet-and-spicy apricot-mustard sauce—so delicious. Not only are these dumplings succulent and flavorful, but the immune-boosting and cancer-fighting properties of fresh ginger and shiitake mushrooms make this a cure-all recipe, too. Have no fear if you were never any good at origami, as these little dumplings are easy to fill and fold . . . and even easier to eat!

APRICOT-MUSTARD SAUCE

½ cup apricot jam   1 tablespoon Dijon mustard

WONTONS

4 tablespoons canola oil, divided   ¼ cup shredded carrots
5 ounces shiitake mushrooms, stemmed   2 cloves garlic, minced
    and sliced   ½ teaspoon grated fresh ginger
½ cup cashews   2 tablespoons soy sauce
2 scallions, trimmed and thinly sliced   Egg-free gyoza or wonton wrappers*

To make the Apricot-Mustard Sauce: Combine jam and mustard in a small saucepan and cook over medium heat for 3 minutes, stirring frequently. Transfer to a small serving bowl and let cool to room temperature.

To make the Wontons: In a large skillet, heat 2 tablespoons oil over medium-high heat, and sauté mushrooms until soft and lightly browned. Stir in cashews, scallions, carrots, garlic, ginger, and soy sauce. Let cook 5 more minutes until fragrant. Set aside to cool slightly. Transfer mixture to a food processor and pulse until cashews are finely ground and mixture is somewhat smooth.

Place 2 teaspoons of the mushroom mixture in the center of each wrapper and moisten the edges of the wrapper with water. As you fold the wrapper in half to enclose the filling, squeeze out as much air as possible to avoid air pockets. If you want to be fancy, fold little

*If you can't find these at your local grocery store, you can find them at an Asian market.

(continued on next page)

pleats along the top side of the dumpling before pinching together to seal. Otherwise, just seal it.

Heat remaining 2 tablespoons oil in a large nonstick skillet over medium-high heat. When oil is hot, arrange the dumplings in the skillet. Do not overcrowd them. Cook the dumplings for a few minutes until the bottoms are lightly browned, checking by lifting each dumpling with a spatula.

Being very careful to avoid spattering oil, slowly fill the skillet with ½ inch hot water. Cover immediately and let cook for approximately 5 minutes, or until all of the water has evaporated. Flip the dumplings and cook for another few minutes in the remaining oil, until the other side is lightly browned as well. Arrange on a platter and serve with Apricot-Mustard Sauce.

Note: If you would prefer to steam the dumplings, fill a large pot with enough water to reach the bottom of a steamer basket. Place the dumplings in the basket, cover, and steam for 15 minutes. Check the pot occasionally and add more water if necessary.

Soups and Salads

Caesar Salad
with Maple-Wheat Croutons

SERVES 6 TO 8

When my friends from Italy come to visit, the first meal on their California to-eat list is always Caesar salad. This never made any sense to me until I learned that Caesar salad does not exist in Italy: It was invented in a restaurant in Tijuana in the 1920s by Italian chef Caesar Cardini. I guess it never made it across the Atlantic! Here is my delicious, creamy, and not-so-Italian salad.

Make-Ahead Tip

The Caesar Dressing can be made 2 to 3 days in advance and kept refrigerated. The Maple-Wheat Croutons can be kept sealed in the freezer for up to 1 month.

MAPLE-WHEAT CROUTONS

6 slices whole-wheat bread, cut into
    ½-inch cubes
¼ cup olive oil
1 tablespoon maple syrup

½ teaspoon sea salt
¼ teaspoon freshly ground black
    pepper

CAESAR DRESSING

¼ cup soft tofu
¼ cup olive oil
2 cloves garlic
2 tablespoons lemon juice
1 tablespoon white or apple-cider
    vinegar

1 tablespoon Dijon mustard
1 tablespoon white miso paste
1 teaspoon sea salt
½ teaspoon freshly ground black
    pepper

1 head romaine lettuce, cut or torn into
    bite-sized pieces

2 tablespoons drained capers

To make the Maple-Wheat Croutons: **Preheat the oven to 325 degrees.**

(continued on next page)

Caesar Salad with Maple-Wheat Croutons (*cont.*)

In a large bowl, toss bread cubes with oil, maple syrup, salt, and pepper. Spread the bread cubes in one layer onto a rimmed baking sheet. Bake for 25 to 35 minutes until crisp and lightly browned, turning with a spatula every ten minutes.

To make the Caesar Dressing: In a blender or food processor, combine tofu, oil, garlic, lemon juice, vinegar, mustard, miso, salt, and pepper. Process until very smooth.

In a large bowl, combine lettuce and capers, and toss with desired amount of Caesar Dressing. Top with a handful of Maple-Wheat Croutons.

California Chipotle Chop
with Agave-Lime Vinaigrette

SERVES 6 AS A SIDE SALAD, 4 AS A MEAL

I don't usually consider salad to be a real meal in itself, but this is an exception. This hearty chopped salad showcases California's finest ingredients with a touch of south-of-the-border flavor. Loaded with goodies like spiced black beans, protein-packed quinoa, and hunks of avocado, this salad won't leave you hungry.

AGAVE-LIME VINAIGRETTE

3 tablespoons olive oil

2 tablespoons apple-cider vinegar

2 tablespoons agave

¼ cup lime juice

CHIPOTLE CHOP

1 tablespoon olive oil

1 15-ounce can black beans, rinsed and drained

1 clove garlic, minced

¼ teaspoon chipotle chili powder

½ teaspoon sea salt

1 head romaine lettuce, cut or torn into bite-sized pieces

1 large tomato, finely chopped

¼ red onion, finely chopped

1 avocado, pitted, peeled, and diced, see Tip (page 32)

½ cup cooked quinoa

2 tablespoons finely chopped fresh cilantro

To make the Agave-Lime Vinaigrette: Blend oil, vinegar, agave, and lime juice in a blender until smooth. Set aside.

To make the Chipotle Chop: Heat oil in a small saucepan over medium heat, and sauté black beans, garlic, chipotle powder, and salt for 5 minutes. Let cool.

In a large bowl, combine romaine, tomatoes, onions, avocado, quinoa, black bean mixture, and cilantro. Toss with desired amount of Agave-Lime Vinaigrette.

Cheesy Broccoli Soup
in Sourdough Bread Bowls

SERVES 8

This soup has a smooth cheesy base with hearty chunks of tender broccoli. I always turn to this recipe when I'm in need of a cozy comfort-food fix. This dish is a perfect cure for rainy-day blues. Served in a crusty sourdough bread bowl? Yes, please!

2 tablespoons olive oil, plus extra for
    brushing
1 onion, chopped
Sea salt
2 cloves garlic, minced
2 cups vegetable broth
2 cups soy, almond, or rice milk

1 bunch broccoli, florets cut, stems
    trimmed, peeled, and chopped
¾ cup nutritional yeast flakes
2 teaspoons lemon juice
Freshly ground black pepper
8 regular sourdough loaves or 16
    small sourdough breads

Preheat the oven to 350 degrees.

In a large pot, heat 2 tablespoons oil over medium-high heat, and sauté onions until soft. Season generously with salt, add garlic, and let cook a few more minutes.

Add broth, nondairy milk, and broccoli. Bring to a simmer, cover, reduce heat to medium-low and let simmer for 20 minutes until broccoli is tender.

Spoon out a small amount of broccoli florets and reserve. In batches, transfer the remaining contents of the pot to a blender and puree. Return pureed soup to the pot and add the reserved broccoli florets. Over low heat, stir in nutritional yeast until incorporated. Add lemon juice and season with salt and pepper. Mix well.

Slice the tops off each sourdough bread; and using a spoon and/or knife, hollow out the inside. Cut or tear the removed bread into bite-sized chunks and set aside. Brush oil on the inside of each bowl to seal the bread so that the soup will not leak out. Place bread bowls on a baking sheet and bake for 15 minutes, or until lightly browned on the inside. Remove from oven and place each bread bowl into a soup bowl. Ladle the soup into the bread bowl and serve with the bread chunks.

Chloe's Favorite Five-Minute Salad

SERVES 6

This salad takes all of five minutes to make and uses only five ingredients. The avocado fuses with the rice vinegar to form a sweet and creamy dressing with no added oil. It is my all-time favorite salad, not only because it is so easy to make, but also because the flavors and textures are perfectly balanced.

4 ounces mixed greens

1 large tomato, chopped

2 scallions, trimmed and thinly sliced

1 avocado, pitted and peeled

4 tablespoons seasoned rice vinegar, as needed

Sea salt

Freshly ground black pepper

In a large bowl, combine greens, tomatoes, scallions, and avocado. Drizzle 1 to 2 tablespoons of vinegar and mix the salad together, mashing the avocado as you toss. I usually wear gloves and use my hands for this step, but you could make it work with a large spoon. Season with salt and pepper to taste. If you want more tanginess, add more vinegar, 1 tablespoon at a time.

Curried Lentil, Squash, and Apple Stew

SERVES 6

Infused with curry spices and chock full of wilted spinach, butternut squash, and sweet chunks of apple, this unique lentil stew is fragrant and flavorful beyond belief.

2 tablespoons olive oil
1 onion, diced
1 carrot, peeled and diced
3 cloves garlic, minced
1 teaspoon grated fresh ginger
1 tablespoon curry powder
1½ teaspoons sea salt

½ cup dried lentils
2½ cups vegetable broth
2 tablespoons tomato paste
3 cups peeled butternut squash
   (½-inch cubes)
1 large unpeeled apple, diced
5 ounces baby spinach

In a large pot, heat oil over medium-high heat, and sauté onions and carrots until almost soft. Add garlic, ginger, curry, and salt, and let cook a few more minutes until fragrant. Stir in lentils, broth, and tomato paste. Bring to boil, cover, and simmer for 25 minutes. Add squash and apples, cover, and simmer for another 25 minutes, or until vegetables and lentils are tender. Uncover and stir in spinach until wilted. Add salt to taste and serve.

Easy Peasy Pasta Salad

SERVES 8 TO 10

This is my mom's family's pasta salad recipe, which we veganized, and serve at every Coscarelli occasion. Wedding showers, birthdays, Halloween parties, or barbecues—this pasta salad is always invited and enjoyed to the very last wheel. A potato is the secret ingredient to give body to the creamy salmon-colored sauce that coats each noodle. I like using this pasta shape because the green peas get caught in the spokes of the wheel. Many friends and family members who have dined at our home have asked me for the recipe, so I will finally reveal it here.

Make-Ahead Tip
Sauce can be made 2 to 3 days in advance and kept refrigerated.

1 small new potato, red or white, peeled and quartered	1 tablespoon drained capers
1 pound wagon wheel pasta	1 tablespoon dried oregano
1½ cups frozen peas	1 teaspoon dried basil
1 clove garlic	1 heaping teaspoon sea salt
3 tablespoons tomato paste	½ cup cold water
2 tablespoons Dijon mustard	⅔ cup olive oil

Place potato in a small saucepan and cover with salted water. Bring to a boil and let cook until tender. Drain, rinse with cold water, and let potatoes cool completely.

Bring a large pot of heavily salted water to a boil. Add wagon wheels and cook according to package directions. Add frozen peas to the boiling pasta right before draining. Drain, rinse with cold water, and drain again. Transfer pasta and peas to a large serving bowl.

Meanwhile, combine cooled potatoes, garlic, tomato paste, mustard, capers, oregano, basil, salt, and water in a food processor. Slowly add the oil in a thin stream and process until smooth. Toss pasta and peas with sauce, and adjust seasoning to taste. Serve at room temperature or chilled.

Mandarin Peanut-Crunch Salad with Crispy Wontons

SERVES 6

It's always a big scene ordering Chinese chicken salad at a restaurant because I have to ask the waiter to hold the chicken, hold the egg wontons; I might as well ask him to hold the entire salad. In my pumped-up vegan version of the popular restaurant salad, I combine crisp cabbage, juicy Mandarin oranges, crunchy peanuts, and homemade wontons tossed with a sweet and tangy dressing. Who needs the chicken?

DRESSING

¼ cup rice vinegar

2 tablespoons canola oil

2 tablespoons brown sugar

1 tablespoon orange marmalade

1¼ teaspoons chili-garlic sauce

CRISPY WONTONS

Egg-free gyoza or wonton wrappers*

Canola oil for frying

4 ounces mixed greens of choice

1 cup shredded red cabbage

¼ cup shredded carrot

1 scallion, trimmed and thinly sliced

1 11-ounce can Mandarin orange segments, drained

½ cup chopped roasted peanuts

To make the dressing: In a blender, process vinegar, oil, brown sugar, marmalade, and chili-garlic sauce until smooth. Adjust sweetness to taste.

To make the Crispy Wontons: Using a pizza cutter or sharp knife, cut each wrapper into ¼-inch strips. Fill a small skillet with ½ inch oil and heat over medium heat until a small piece of wrapper sizzles when dropped into the oil. Gently place wonton strips into the heated oil and fry until crisp, about 15 to 20 seconds, watching very carefully so that they don't burn. Drain on paper towels.

In a large bowl, combine greens, cabbage, carrots, scallions, oranges, and peanuts. Toss with desired amount of dressing and top with a handful of Crispy Wontons.

*If you can't find these at your local grocery store, you can find them at an Asian market.

Minted Couscous with Arugula, Butternut Squash, and Currants

SERVES 8

This light and fresh couscous salad is the perfect blend of a green salad and a pasta salad, since couscous is technically a pasta! Israeli couscous, also known as pearl couscous, is my favorite variety of couscous because it is large and plump, which adds a nice bite to the salad. In this recipe, I combine the couscous with sweet roasted butternut squash, currants, peppery arugula, fresh fragrant mint, and toasted almonds for a little crunch. Lightly tossed with olive oil, this salad is simple perfection and can be enjoyed as a light lunch or side dish.

4 tablespoons olive oil, divided
3 cups ½-inch cubes peeled butternut
    squash
Sea salt
Freshly ground black pepper
2 cups Israeli pearl couscous

2½ cups vegetable broth
1 cup arugula
¼ cup currants
½ cup slivered almonds, toasted
2 tablespoons finely chopped fresh
    mint

Preheat the oven to 375 degrees.

In a large bowl, toss 2 tablespoons oil with squash and season generously with salt and pepper. Transfer to a large rimmed baking sheet and roast for 30 to 35 minutes until squash is fork tender, turning once or twice with a spatula. Let cool.

In the meantime, combine 1 tablespoon oil, couscous, 1 teaspoon salt, and broth in a medium saucepan. Bring to a boil; reduce heat and simmer, covered, for 10 minutes until tender. Remove from heat and let sit, covered, for 5 minutes, or until all liquid has been absorbed. Toss couscous with remaining 1 tablespoon oil and spread on a large rimmed baking sheet to cool.

Toss cooled couscous with cooled butternut squash, arugula, currants, almonds, and mint. Adjust seasoning to taste and serve.

Simple Side Salad
with Shallot-Dijon Vinaigrette

SERVES 6

Having a bowl of fresh greens and garden vegetables tossed with a flavorful vinaigrette is often the perfect way to enhance your meal without upstaging the main course. This is my go-to side salad when I am serving a heavy entrée and need something to lighten the meal. Feel free to be creative with your add-ons and make this salad as complex, or as simple, as you'd like. For a shortcut, grab your salad fixings from a salad bar.

SHALLOT-DIJON VINAIGRETTE

⅓ cup olive oil

2 tablespoons apple cider vinegar

1 teaspoon Dijon mustard

1 medium shallot, thinly sliced

¼ teaspoon sea salt

4 ounces mixed greens of choice

1 large tomato, chopped

3 tablespoons peeled and shredded carrots

3 tablespoons peeled and shredded beets

¼ cucumber, very thinly sliced

2 tablespoons chopped fresh Italian parsley

Freshly ground black pepper

To make the Shallot-Dijon Vinaigrette: Combine oil, vinegar, mustard, shallots, and salt in a blender, and process until combined.

In a large bowl, combine greens, tomatoes, carrots, beets, cucumbers, and parsley. Toss with desired amount of Shallot-Dijon Vinaigrette, and season with pepper before serving.

Tomato-Basil Bisque
with Pumpernickel Croutons

SERVES 6

The first thing that my brother Andy said when I served him this was, "I forgot how much I love soup." I scribbled down his words on the recipe to remind me that this soup was a huge success. The tomatoes are roasted with onions and garlic at a high heat until they caramelize. The caramelized vegetables are then pureed with fresh basil into a smooth bisque. Served with crunchy homemade croutons, this bisque is much more exciting than traditional tomato soup, which I usually find boring. Expect to keep getting up to serve seconds and thirds of this delicious bisque, or better yet, keep the pot on the table.

PUMPERNICKEL CROUTONS

6 slices pumpernickel bread, cut into
   ½-inch cubes
¼ cup olive oil

½ teaspoon sea salt
¼ teaspoon freshly ground black
   pepper

TOMATO-BASIL BISQUE

2 to 2½ pounds tomatoes, quartered
5 cloves garlic, peeled and left whole
2 onions, sliced
¼ cup olive oil
Sea salt
Freshly ground black pepper

2 cups vegetable broth
½ cup chopped fresh basil, plus extra
   for chiffonade garnish, see Tip
   (page 77)
2 tablespoons brown sugar
1 teaspoon lemon juice

To make the Pumpernickel Croutons: Preheat the oven to 325 degrees.

In a large bowl, toss bread cubes with oil, salt, and pepper. Spread the bread cubes in one layer onto a rimmed baking sheet. Bake for 25 to 35 minutes until crisp and lightly browned, turning with a spatula every 10 minutes.

To make the Tomato-Basil Bisque: Preheat the oven to 450 degrees.

(continued on page 65)

Tomato-Basil Bisque with Pumpernickel Croutons (*cont.*)

Spread tomatoes, garlic, and onions on a large rimmed baking sheet and drizzle with olive oil. Generously season with salt and pepper, then roast for 30 to 35 minutes, or until tomatoes are lightly browned and caramelized.

Transfer roasted vegetables to a large pot and add broth. Bring to a boil, then simmer for 10 minutes. Transfer the soup in small batches to a blender and add basil. Your blender should never be more than half full. You could use an immersion blender if you prefer. Puree until very smooth. Return soup to the pot and mix in brown sugar and lemon juice. Add more salt and pepper to taste. Serve garnished with Pumpernickel Croutons and basil.

Tuscan Bean and Greens Soup over Garlic Toast

SERVES 8

After graduating from college, I traveled around Italy with three of my girlfriends and we ate our way through the country. We all agreed that the best meal of the trip was in Florence at a quaint trattoria where we ate a spectacular soup that inspired this recipe. I know you might think we're crazy for declaring a bowl of soup to be the best meal out of a summer in Italy (hello, pasta?), but it goes to show how good this recipe is!

Hearty cannellini beans with tender wilted escarole, chopped tomatoes, and a kick of red pepper make for a flavorful and colorful bowl. Dip your spoon in to find a sunken piece of crusty garlic bread—surprise! This adds a wow factor and deliciously fills out each spoonful of soup.

TUSCAN BEAN AND GREENS SOUP

- 2 15-ounce cans cannellini or other white beans, rinsed and drained, divided into two bowls
- 3 cups vegetable broth, divided
- 2 tablespoons olive oil
- 1 onion, chopped
- 3 cloves garlic, minced
- ⅛ teaspoon crushed red pepper
- Sea salt
- 1 head escarole, roughly chopped
- 1 large tomato, seeded and finely chopped
- Freshly ground black pepper

GARLIC TOAST

- ¼ cup olive oil
- 3 cloves garlic, pressed
- 8 slices baguette, crust removed

To make the Tuscan Bean and Greens Soup: In a food processor, prepare the bean puree by combining 1 can beans with 1 cup broth, and process until completely smooth. Set aside.

In a large pot, heat oil and sauté onions until soft. Add garlic, red pepper, and ¼ teaspoon sea salt. Stir quickly, then immediately add escarole and stir occasionally, until escarole is soft and wilted. Do not let brown. Add remaining 2 cups broth, tomatoes, remaining 1 can

Chloe's Kitchen

beans, bean puree, and another ¼ teaspoon salt. Cover and bring to a boil. Reduce heat and simmer for 20 minutes. Season with pepper and adjust salt to taste.

To make the Garlic Toast: Preheat the oven to broil.

In a small bowl, mix oil and garlic until combined. Brush each slice of bread on both sides with garlic oil and arrange them on a baking sheet.

Broil for 1 to 2 minutes on each side, or until crisp and lightly browned. Watch the toast carefully; it can burn very quickly.

To serve: Place a slice of Garlic Toast at the bottom of each soup bowl and ladle the Tuscan Bean and Greens Soup on top.

Wasabi Sesame Noodle Salad

SERVES 8

You're either a wasabi person or you're not. Well, I'm actually not a wasabi person and always have to look the other way when my mom eats it straight off her chopstick. However, this noodle salad caters to wasabi lovers and haters alike, because the flavor is very subtle with just a hint of heat. The chilled noodles speckled with black sesame seeds make for a beautiful salad that can be enjoyed by a variety of palates.

10 ounces soba noodles
1 tablespoon toasted sesame oil
3 tablespoons soy sauce
3 tablespoons rice vinegar
1 tablespoon agave
1 teaspoon wasabi powder
2 cloves garlic, minced

1 teaspoon chili-garlic sauce
1 cucumber, peeled and shredded
1 carrot, peeled and shredded
1 scallion, trimmed and thinly sliced
1 tablespoon black sesame seeds
Sea salt

Bring a large pot of heavily salted water to a boil. Add soba noodles and cook according to package directions. Drain, rinse with cold water, and drain again. In a large bowl, toss cooled noodles with oil.

Meanwhile, mix together soy sauce, vinegar, agave, wasabi powder, garlic, and chili-garlic sauce in a small bowl. Stir until wasabi powder is dissolved and all ingredients are combined.

Toss noodles with wasabi mixture, cucumbers, carrots, scallions, and sesame seeds. Add salt if needed, and serve at room temperature or chilled.

. . . .

Chloe's Tip: Shredding Cucumber

Peel the cucumber. Shred each side on a handheld grater, working toward the middle. Stop shredding when you get to the seeds and move on to the next side.

. . . .

Chloe's Kitchen

Simply Vegetables

Classic Roasted Vegetables

SERVES 4 TO 6

You will be amazed by what just a drizzle of olive oil and a pinch of salt and pepper can do to these garden beauties! Roasting at a high heat caramelizes the vegetables and brings out their natural sweetness. Even the pickiest eaters (both kids and adults) ask for seconds of my roasted vegetables because they are simply irresistible! I like to roast cauliflower, broccoli, and carrots, but feel free to use any combination of vegetables and in any amount. As long as the vegetables are coated in olive oil and seasoned well with salt and pepper, you really can't go wrong.

For a shortcut, purchase an assortment of cut raw vegetables.

Make-Ahead Tip

Vegetables can be roasted a day in advance and kept refrigerated. Reheat before serving by roasting at 375 degrees until heated through.

½ head cauliflower, cut into florets

½ bunch broccoli, cut into florets

3 carrots, peeled and cut into bite-sized pieces

¼ to ½ cup olive oil

Sea salt

Freshly ground black pepper

Preheat the oven to 400 degrees.

In a large bowl, toss cut vegetables with enough oil, salt, and pepper to generously coat each piece.

Spread vegetables in one layer on a large rimmed baking sheet. Roast for approximately 45 minutes, stirring and rotating the vegetables every 15 minutes. If they begin to dry out, add more oil and toss. Once all vegetables are fork tender and slightly browned, remove from oven. Adjust seasoning to taste.

Coconut Mashed Yams with Currants

SERVES 6

When I was a baby, my mom noticed my skin turning orange and took me to the doctor. Turns out, I was eating way too many yams, and beta-carotene was the culprit. That's right, I OD'ed on yams. They were my first favorite food and I am still addicted to this day! Lucky for me they are loaded with vitamin B6, vitamin C, potassium, and fiber. In this recipe, I've dressed them up with a hint of creamy coconut and an infusion of warm autumn spices. Every so often, you'll catch a plump currant that will make that bite even better.

3 large garnet or other yams, peeled and cut into 2-inch pieces

1 cup canned coconut milk, mixed well before measuring

⅓ cup maple syrup or packed brown sugar

½ teaspoon sea salt

¼ teaspoon ground cinnamon

¼ teaspoon ground cloves

¼ teaspoon ground ginger

⅓ cup currants, soaked in warm water for 10 to 15 minutes and drained

Place yams in a large pot and cover with cold water. Cover and bring to a boil. Cook until fork tender, 15 to 20 minutes. Drain and return to pot.

Add coconut milk, maple syrup, salt, cinnamon, cloves, and ginger, and mash with a potato masher until smooth. Adjust seasoning to taste. Add more coconut milk for a creamier texture and more maple syrup for a sweeter flavor. Mix in currants and serve.

Fire-Roasted Artichokes with Garlic Oil

SERVES 4

Drizzling the artichoke with balsamic vinegar before grilling adds a tangy, smoky flavor to the vegetable. Plus, dipping the leaves in the Garlic Oil afterward makes them even tastier.

GARLIC OIL

1 head garlic	Sea salt
½ cup plus 1 tablespoon olive oil, divided	Freshly ground black pepper

FIRE-ROASTED ARTICHOKES

2 large artichokes	Sea salt
1 tablespoon olive oil	Freshly ground black pepper
2 tablespoons balsamic vinegar	

To make the Garlic Oil: Preheat the oven to 375 degrees.

Peel away the papery outer layers of the garlic bulb, but leave the individual garlic skins intact. Slice off the pointy end of the head of garlic, so that the tips of all cloves are exposed. Place the head of garlic on foil, cut side up, drizzle with 1 tablespoon oil, and season with salt and pepper. Loosely fold up the ends of the foil pouch and pinch to seal. Roast for 30 to 40 minutes, or until the garlic cloves are fork tender. Remove from the oven and let cool. Once cooled, squeeze the head of garlic and the soft cloves will pop out. In a small bowl, mash the roasted garlic with remaining ½ cup oil and ⅛ teaspoon salt. Set aside.

To make the Fire-Roasted Artichokes: Cut off the stem end of each artichoke and pull off the tough outer leaves. With a sharp knife, cut ¾ inch to 1 inch off the top of each artichoke. Using kitchen shears, cut off the sharp tips of the remaining leaves.

Fill a large pot with enough water to reach the bottom of a steamer basket. Place artichokes in the basket, cover, and steam for about 30 to 45 minutes, or until the bases are fork

(continued on next page)

Fire-Roasted Artichokes with Garlic Oil (*cont.*)

tender. Check the pot occasionally and add more water if necessary. Remove from steam basket and let cool.

Cut each artichoke into halves or quarters. Using a spoon, remove the fuzzy choke. Drizzle with oil and vinegar, and season with salt and pepper.

Preheat a grill or stovetop grill pan.

Place each artichoke piece on the grill cut side down. Grill for 5 minutes, or until each piece is nicely browned. Remove from grill and serve with Garlic Oil.

Chloe's Kitchen

Garlicky Greens

SERVES 4

How could something that's this good for you taste so incredible? With garlic, of course! Kale is a crazy amazing superfood that beats every other vegetable when it comes to nutritional content. Rich in vitamin C, vitamin K, iron, calcium, fiber, potassium, and manganese, this cruciferous leafy green works wonders on the body and contains high levels of antioxidant, anti-inflammatory, and anticancer nutrients. It comes in different varieties, the most common being curly kale which is bright green with curly leaves, and Lacinato kale, aka dinosaur kale, which is dark green-blue and has a more delicate flavor.

Infusing this all-star green vegetable with fresh garlic and a splash of lemon juice makes for a healthful savory side to any meal. There's no such thing as too much kale, so I pair this dish with pretty much everything!

2 tablespoons olive oil	Sea salt
1 bunch kale or other leafy greens, thick stems removed, and cut into chiffonade or torn into bite-sized pieces	Freshly ground black pepper
	4 to 5 cloves garlic, minced
	½ teaspoon lemon juice
	Pinch crushed red pepper, optional

Heat oil in a large skillet over medium-high heat. Add kale in batches, stirring continually. Season with salt and pepper to taste. Once all of the kale has turned bright green and has begun to wilt, add garlic and cook for another minute. You may need to add a tablespoon or two of water if the garlic sticks to the skillet. Remove from heat and toss with lemon juice and red pepper. Adjust seasoning and lemon juice to taste and serve immediately.

. . . .

Chloe's Tip: Chiffonade

Chiffonade means "made of rags." To cut an herb or vegetable in chiffonade, first stack the leaves as evenly as you can. Roll the stack tightly so it resembles a cigar. Slice the roll crosswise into very thin slices, and pull apart the slices into strips. A chiffonade of basil is used quite often as a garnish.

. . . .

Grilled Lemon–Olive Oil Asparagus

SERVES 4

Did you know that asparagus grows seven inches a day when the weather is warm? No wonder that sunny California is the leading producer of the crop! Fresh spears will have dark green and purple tips and the ends should be freshly cut, not dried out. I find myself popping these grilled asparagus spears in my mouth as if they were French fries, and I'll bet you will, too.

1 bunch asparagus, ends trimmed, see Tip (page 139)	Sea salt
2 tablespoons olive oil	Freshly ground black pepper
1 teaspoon lemon zest	1 lemon, halved

Preheat a grill or stovetop grill pan.

Toss asparagus with 2 tablespoons oil and lemon zest. Season with salt and pepper to taste.

Place asparagus on the hot grill perpendicular to the grates so that they do not fall through. Grill asparagus for about 5 minutes, rolling each spear every minute to ensure even browning on all sides. Remove from grill and place on a platter. Squeeze lemon over the asparagus. Adjust seasoning to taste with salt and pepper.

Note: If you do not want to grill, roast the asparagus in the oven at 400 degrees for about 10 to 15 minutes until fork tender and ends are slightly crispy.

Guilt-Free Garlic Mashed Potatoes

This healthful gourmet version of mashed potatoes is the most delicious trick in the book! You can make this recipe using any combination or proportion of potatoes, parsnips, and cauliflower. Use only cauliflower for the lowest-calorie option or five russet potatoes for old-fashioned mashed potatoes. I enjoy combining all three vegetables, but the choice is yours. No matter what you use, this is a creamy and delicious side dish with a mild roasted garlic flavor that can serve as a fluffy bed for any entrée. Fear not that you are using a whole head of garlic; roasting garlic mellows its pungency. Mmmmm . . . mellow garlicky mashed magic!

1 head garlic
1 tablespoon olive oil
Sea salt
Freshly ground black pepper
2 russet potatoes, peeled and cut into
    2-inch pieces

2 medium parsnips, peeled and cut
    into 2-inch pieces
1 head cauliflower, cut into florets
¼ cup soy, almond, or rice milk, or
    vegetable stock
2 tablespoons vegan margarine or
    olive oil

Preheat the oven to 375 degrees.

Peel away the papery outer layers of the garlic bulb, but leave the individual garlic skins intact. Slice off the pointy end of the head of garlic, so that the tips of all cloves are exposed. Place the head of garlic on foil, cut side up, and drizzle with oil and season with salt and pepper. Loosely fold up the ends of the foil pouch and pinch to seal. Roast for 30 to 40 minutes until the garlic cloves are fork tender. Remove from the oven and let cool. Once cooled, squeeze the head of garlic and the soft cloves will pop out. Set aside.

While the garlic is roasting, place potatoes, parsnips, and cauliflower in a large pot and cover with cold water. Generously salt the water, cover, and bring to a boil. Boil until vegetables are fork tender. Drain and return to pot.

Add the roasted garlic, nondairy milk, and margarine; mash together. Season to taste with salt and pepper and add more nondairy milk or margarine as needed.

Maple-Roasted Brussels Sprouts with Toasted Hazelnuts

SERVES 6

Forget all your notions of what Brussels sprouts taste like. These little gems are roasted at a high heat to bring out the natural sugars and caramelize the outer leaves. They are tossed with toasty hazelnuts and a splash of maple syrup to turn them from ordinary to extraordinary. These cancer-fighting cruciferous Brussels sprouts are packed with vitamin C, potassium, and fiber, but they taste just like candy!

Make-Ahead Tip

Brussels sprouts can be roasted a day in advance and kept refrigerated. Reheat before serving by roasting at 375 degrees until heated through.

1½ pounds Brussels sprouts	2 tablespoons maple syrup
¼ cup olive oil	½ cup coarsely chopped hazelnuts,
¾ teaspoon sea salt	toasted (see Tip, page 82)
¼ teaspoon black pepper	

Preheat the oven to 375 degrees.

To prepare Brussels sprouts, remove any yellow or brown outer leaves, cut off the stems, and cut in half. In a large bowl, toss the Brussels sprouts, oil, salt, and pepper together. Once all of the Brussels sprouts are coated in oil, arrange them in a 9 x 13-inch pan.

Roast for 15 minutes. Stir Brussels sprouts around with a spatula or large spoon to even out the browning; continue to roast for another 30 minutes. Stir the Brussels sprouts again, and drizzle maple syrup over top. Roast the Brussels sprouts for about 15 minutes more, or until they are fork tender (about 45 minutes total roasting time).

Toss the roasted Brussels sprouts with the hazelnuts and serve.

(continued on next page)

Maple Roasted Brussels Sprouts with Toasted Hazelnuts (*cont.*)

. . . .

Chloe's Tip: Toasting Hazelnuts

To toast the hazelnuts: Preheat oven to 350 degrees. Place the hazelnuts in one layer on a rimmed baking sheet. Roast for 10 to 12 minutes, or until lightly browned and fragrant. Keep checking on them every few minutes because nuts can burn quickly.

. . . .

Teriyaki Wok Vegetables

SERVES 4 TO 6

A lot of bottled teriyaki sauces are filled with high-fructose corn syrup and artificial colors, but who needs 'em? This all-natural sauce will leave you licking your lips or even the plate! This dish is best served over rice or tossed with soba noodles.

TERIYAKI SAUCE

¾ cup water

3 tablespoons soy sauce

½ teaspoon grated fresh ginger

1 clove garlic, minced

2 tablespoons brown sugar or maple syrup

1 tablespoon cornstarch or arrowroot

WOK VEGETABLES

2 tablespoons canola oil

1 large carrot, peeled and thinly cut on the diagonal

1 head bok choy, ends trimmed, thinly sliced on the diagonal

1 small red onion, thinly sliced

¼ pound mushrooms of choice, stemmed and thinly sliced

1 cup half-moon sliced zucchini

4 ounces snow peas, strings removed

1 tablespoon toasted sesame oil

To make the Teriyaki sauce: In a medium saucepan, whisk together water, soy sauce, ginger, garlic, brown sugar, and cornstarch. Heat the sauce over medium-high heat, whisking frequently, until it comes to a boil. Reduce the heat to medium-low and cook, whisking frequently, until the mixture has thickened and big syrupy bubbles appear on the surface.

To prepare the Wok Vegetables: In a large wok or skillet, heat canola oil over medium-high heat and add carrots, bok choy, onions, mushrooms, and zucchini. Using tongs, stir-fry vegetables until they begin to soften and turn bright in color, about 10 to 15 minutes. Add enough Teriyaki Sauce to coat the vegetables and let cook a few minutes more. Once vegetables are fork tender, stir in snow peas and sesame oil. Remove from heat and serve over rice or tossed with soba noodles.

Miso-Glazed Eggplant

SERVES 6

Nasu dengaku, *Japanese for Miso-Glazed Eggplant, is a very popular dish in Japan and in my kitchen. Miso is a fermented soy paste, rich in protein and B vitamins, with amazing healing and immune-boosting qualities. There are many different varieties of miso. I prefer to use a mellow white or yellow miso for this recipe because both are sweet and mild in flavor.*

While most recipes for this traditional dish require a long list of Asian ingredients, my recipe is extremely simple with just a three-ingredient glaze. It comes together in seconds and will disappear off the plate in about the same time without so much as a "sayonara"! Serve as a side dish or over rice.

2 tablespoons water	3 Japanese eggplant (about 1½
¼ cup agave	pounds), stem ends removed, cut
2 tablespoons white miso paste	into ½-inch slices on the diagonal
2 tablespoons sesame oil	2 scallions, trimmed and thinly sliced
	Toasted sesame seeds, for garnish

Preheat the oven to broil. Lightly grease a medium baking sheet.

In a small saucepan, whisk together water and agave over medium-high heat until boiling. Let boil for 1 to 2 minutes, then reduce heat to low. Add miso and whisk until smooth. Turn off heat and let cool until mixture thickens.

In the meantime, heat sesame oil in a large skillet over medium heat. Place the eggplant slices into the hot oil in one layer; do not crowd the pan. You may have to cook them in batches, adding more oil as needed. Sauté eggplant until soft and lightly browned on each side, about 2 minutes per side. Transfer eggplant to prepared baking sheet in a single layer and let cool while you cook the remaining eggplant.

Brush each sautéed eggplant slice with miso glaze and broil for 1 minute. Remove from oven and garnish each slice with scallions and sesame seeds.

Sea Salt and Vinegar French Fries

SERVES 4

Sea salt and vinegar potato chips are my guilty pleasure. That salty and tangy combination is always calling to me, so I decided to make a fry-free real potato version. Rejoice French fry lovers! These oven-baked fries are nearly fat free, but still have those crispy salty edges that we all know and love. If you prefer to play it safe, omit the vinegar for traditional fries.

2 large russet potatoes, peeled and cut
    into ¼-inch fries
1 to 2 tablespoons olive oil
Sea salt

Malt vinegar for drizzling
Sweet Tomato Ketchup (page 253),
    optional

Preheat the oven to 400 degrees. Lightly grease a large rimmed baking sheet.

In a large bowl, submerge potato sticks in cold water and let soak for 15 minutes. Drain potato sticks and pat dry thoroughly with a paper towel.

Transfer potato sticks to the prepared baking sheet in one layer and drizzle with enough oil to lightly coat each stick. Season with salt and bake for 30 to 40 minutes, or until evenly browned with crispy edges. Be sure to turn with a spatula occasionally. Remove from oven and lightly drizzle the vinegar onto the fries to taste. Season with more salt to taste and serve with Sweet Tomato Ketchup.

Thyme for Creamy Scalloped Potatoes

SERVES 6 TO 8

This is my mom's no-longer-secret recipe for the best scalloped potatoes in the world, gone vegan. The rich cashew cream blankets thinly sliced potatoes that are baked to perfection with a crispy top. Flecked with sliced scallions and fresh thyme leaves, this dish will amaze even the most discerning cream-sauce connoisseur. I usually eat it straight from the pan because I'd rather burn my tongue than have to wait even a few minutes to eat it from a plate!

1 cup raw cashews*

2 cups water

3 cloves garlic

2 teaspoons sea salt

2 teaspoons fresh thyme leaves, plus extra for garnish

2 scallions, trimmed and thinly sliced

5 russet potatoes, peeled and thinly sliced

Paprika

Preheat the oven to 375 degrees. Lightly grease a 9 x 13-inch pan.

In a blender, puree cashews, water, garlic, and salt. Transfer to a large bowl. Add thyme and scallions to the cashew cream and mix with a spoon. In the pan, arrange half of the sliced potatoes, overlapping, and pour half of the cashew cream on top. Repeat for the second layer. Dust the top with paprika and cover the pan with foil. Bake for 45 minutes. Remove foil and continue baking another 15 minutes, or until potatoes are fork tender and lightly browned on top. Garnish with fresh thyme before serving and adjust salt to taste.

*If you are not using a high-powered blender, such as a Vitamix, soak cashews overnight or boil cashews for 10 minutes and drain. This will soften the cashews and ensure a silky, smooth cream.

Vegetable Tempura

SERVES 10 TO 12

In college, my friends and I would throw tempura parties where we would make a tub of batter, buy tons of veggies, and fry–dip–eat to our hearts' content! This foolproof recipe is supereasy and proves that you don't need to go to a Japanese restaurant to enjoy an authentic platter of Vegetable Tempura. Invite your friends over and let the crispy, dippy yumminess begin!

DIPPING SAUCE

1 cup water

3 tablespoons soy sauce

3 tablespoons mirin

1 tablespoon agave or sugar

1 scallion, trimmed and thinly sliced

VEGETABLE TEMPURA

2 cups all-purpose flour

1 tablespoon baking powder

2 teaspoons sea salt

2 tablespoons sesame oil

2¼ cups ice water

4 to 6 cups assorted vegetables:
  broccoli florets, sliced carrot,
  whole mushrooms, green beans,
  peeled and sliced potato and/or
  sweet potato, asparagus spears
Canola oil for frying

To make the dipping sauce: In a medium saucepan, combine water, soy sauce, mirin, and agave. Bring to a boil and let simmer 5 minutes. Remove from heat and stir in scallions.

To make the Vegetable Tempura: Whisk together flour, baking powder, and salt in a large bowl. In a separate bowl, whisk sesame oil and water. Pour the wet mixture into the dry mixture and whisk until it forms a thin batter. Some lumps are okay. Store in the refrigerator until you are ready to fry.

Fill a deep-sided heavy skillet or deep fryer with about 2 inches of oil. Heat to 350 degrees, or until a small drop of batter sizzles when added to the oil. Dip vegetables in batter and gently place in oil. Oil should sizzle around the vegetables. Let each vegetable fry for about 45 seconds to 1 minute, turning halfway through, until crispy and lightly browned on the outside. Drain on paper towels. Repeat this process for all vegetables. Enjoy immediately with the dipping sauce.

Under-the-Sea Vegetables

SERVES 6 TO 8

Sea vegetables are tasty seaweed plants that soak up incredible minerals and nutrients from the ocean. I eat them at least once a week because they are rich in calcium, iron, zinc, fiber, protein, and iodine, and promote strong bones and healthy thyroid function. My favorite sea vegetables are arame and hijiki because they have the highest nutritional content and have a deliciously salty and chewy bite to them. You can toss leftovers into a salad or stir-fry for a boost of flavor.

1 cup (2 ounces) dried arame or hijiki
2 tablespoons canola oil
1 small onion, chopped
¼ cup shredded carrot

2 tablespoons soy sauce
1 teaspoon lemon juice
1 teaspoon maple syrup

Soak and drain seaweed according to package directions. This process reconstitutes the seaweed so that it is plump.

In a small saucepan, heat oil over medium-high heat and sauté onions until soft. Add seaweed, carrots, and soy sauce. Mix well and continue cooking for about 5 minutes. Stir in lemon juice and maple syrup. Remove from heat and adjust seasoning to taste. Serve warm or chilled.

Eat with Your Hands

Avocado Toast

SERVES 2

While I was attending culinary school in New York City, my classmate Shana, who always knows the hippest eats in town, introduced me to the delicious avocado bread at Café Gitane in SoHo. The California girl in me would head there often to satisfy my uncontrollable avocado cravings. If you are an avocado freak like me, you will love this delectable open-faced sandwich inspired by the charming New York cafe. The best part? The recipe is so simple that there's no measuring necessary!

2 slices multigrain or sourdough bread, toasted

1 avocado, pitted, peeled, and very thinly sliced, see Tip (page 32)

Olive oil

Lemon juice

Sea salt

Freshly ground black pepper

Crushed red pepper

Fan avocado slices on toast and drizzle with olive oil and lemon juice. Season with salt, pepper, and red pepper to taste.

BBQ Pineapple Pizza

SERVES 4

Nothing beats warm pizza crust slathered in tangy BBQ sauce and topped with BBQ baked tofu, caramelized onions, fresh pineapple, and a touch of cilantro. The colors of this pizza are gorgeous and the flavors are insanely good! Keep in mind that this pizza does take some time to make, but the results are well worth it.

For a shortcut, use a bottle of barbeque sauce and store-bought pizza dough.

1 14-ounce package extra-firm tofu, drained

2 cups barbecue sauce, purchased or prepared following recipe on page 254, divided

3 tablespoons olive oil, plus extra for brushing

2 large onions, sliced

Sea salt and freshly ground black pepper

1 to 1½ pounds pizza dough, purchased or prepared following recipe on page 250

1 cup diced pineapple

2 tablespoons chopped fresh cilantro

Preheat the oven to 325 degrees. Lightly grease a small baking sheet.

Press the tofu according to directions on page 252. After pressing, cut the tofu into ½-inch cubes. In a bowl, toss tofu with 1 cup barbecue sauce until each cube is coated. Place in one layer on the prepared baking sheet. Bake for 45 minutes, turning the tofu a couple of times with a spatula. Remove from oven and set aside. Turn heat up to 450 degrees.

In a large skillet, heat 3 tablespoons oil and sauté onions over medium heat until tender and caramelized, about 20 to 30 minutes. Season generously with salt and pepper and set aside.

Brush a large rimmed baking sheet (approximately 9 x 13-inch) with oil.

Stretch pizza dough into a rectangle and fit it into the prepared baking sheet. Spoon remaining 1 cup barbecue sauce onto the pizza dough and spread, leaving a ¾-inch border along the sides. You may not want to use all of the sauce, just enough to coat the dough. On top of the sauce, layer the tofu, caramelized onions, pineapple, and cilantro. Brush the edges of the crust with olive oil. Bake for about 15 to 20 minutes, rotating midway, until the crust is slightly browned or golden. Let cool, slice, and devour!

Grilled Pesto Pizza with Sweet Potatoes, Kale, and Balsamic Reduction

SERVES 6

Think outside the pizza box with this cheeseless creation. Grilling pizza creates nice grill marks on the crust, which makes for a unique presentation and fancy brick oven effect. I know the topping combination here may sound avant-garde, but trust me, it really works and everyone loves it. This far-from-delivery pizza will leave you feeling like a rock star chef as the compliments roll in. Double the Pesto Sauce and toss it with some hot pasta for an Italiano feast. Buonissimo!

Make-Ahead Tip
The Pesto Sauce can be made in advance and kept refrigerated for 2 to 3 days. The sweet potatoes can be roasted in advance and kept refrigerated for 3 to 4 days.

BALSAMIC REDUCTION
1 cup balsamic vinegar

1 tablespoon maple syrup

PESTO SAUCE
2 cups fresh basil

1¼ cups walnuts, toasted

3 cloves garlic

2 tablespoons lemon juice

¾ teaspoon sea salt

½ teaspoon freshly ground black pepper

⅔ cup olive oil

PIZZA TOPPING
1 large red-skinned sweet potato, peeled and cut into ½-inch pieces

5 tablespoons olive oil, divided, plus extra for brushing

Sea salt

½ bunch kale, thick stems removed, and cut into chiffonade or torn into bite-sized pieces

Freshly ground black pepper

1 to 1½ pounds pizza dough, purchased or prepared following recipe on page 250

Flour for rolling

To make the Balsamic Reduction: In a small pan, cook vinegar over medium-low heat until it comes to a boil. Reduce heat and simmer for 20 minutes, or until it reduces to a thick syrup-like consistency. Remove from heat and mix in maple syrup.

To make the Pesto Sauce: In a food processor, combine basil, walnuts, garlic, lemon juice, salt, and pepper. As you process, slowly drizzle in the oil.

To make the pizza topping: Preheat the oven to 350 degrees. Preheat a grill or stovetop grill pan to medium-high heat.

Toss sweet potatoes with 3 tablespoons oil and season with salt. Spread sweet potatoes on a rimmed baking sheet and bake for 20 to 30 minutes, or until fork tender and lightly browned. Be sure to check the sweet potatoes and turn with a spatula frequently.

In a large skillet, heat remaining 2 tablespoons oil over medium-high heat. Add kale, and season with salt and pepper. Sauté kale until wilted and bright green and adjust seasoning to taste. Turn off heat and set aside.

To assemble and grill the pizzas: Cut the dough into six equal pieces. On a lightly floured surface, roll each piece of dough into a 6-inch circle. The circle should be as thin as a tortilla. Lightly brush both sides of the dough circle with oil and grill for about 3 to 5 minutes on one side, until the bottom is lightly browned. Using tongs, flip the dough and immediately spread pesto on the already-browned side and layer sautéed kale and roasted sweet potatoes. Let cook on grill for another 3 to 5 minutes and remove from heat. Repeat this process with remaining dough.

To serve: Drizzle the Balsamic Reduction over the grilled pizzas and serve immediately.

Chloe's Award-Winning Mango Masala Panini

SERVES 4 TO 6

Believe it or not, my entire career began with these panini. Right after graduating culinary school, I entered a local panini-off that was judged by food bloggers and firemen at Coral Tree Café in Los Angeles. My Indian-inspired vegan panini made with Spiced Chickpea Masala, Roasted Cauliflower Curry, and Tamarind-Mango Chutney competed against four other meaty panini stuffed with Swiss cheese, prosciutto, and buttery bacon. I was really nervous considering that firemen are known for their carnivorous appetites, so it was a huge honor and total shock to take home first prize. And it was great to watch the firemen shovel down my panini like doughnuts! I have a video of my parents and brother screaming at the tops of their lungs as my name was called as the winner, and it makes me tear up every time I watch it. I hope this panini recipe is as special for you as it is for me!

Make-Ahead Tip

All components of this recipe can be made in advance and kept refrigerated for 3 to 4 days.

TAMARIND-MANGO CHUTNEY

1 cup diced mango, fresh or frozen

2 tablespoons brown sugar

1 teaspoon tamarind paste

2 tablespoons water

SPICED CHICKPEA MASALA

2 tablespoons olive oil

1 onion, chopped

Sea salt

3 garlic cloves, minced

1 teaspoon grated fresh ginger

1 teaspoon ground turmeric

½ teaspoon ground cumin

½ teaspoon ground cinnamon

½ teaspoon ground cloves

1 large pinch cayenne

1 15-ounce can chickpeas, rinsed
    and drained

2 tomatoes, finely chopped

½ cup water

Freshly ground black pepper

¼ cup finely chopped fresh cilantro

1 tablespoon brown sugar or maple
    syrup

2 teaspoons lemon juice

(continued on next page)

Roasted Cauliflower Curry (page 38)   ½ cup spinach
4 ciabatta rolls, sliced in half, or 8 slices   Olive oil for brushing
    sandwich bread

Preheat panini press to high.

To make the Tamarind-Mango Chutney: Combine mango, brown sugar, tamarind, and water in a medium saucepan. Cook over medium-low heat for about 10 minutes, or until mango is tender. Pulse a few times in food processor so that mixture is spreadable yet chunky, and store in refrigerator.

To make the Spiced Chickpea Masala: In a large skillet, heat oil and sauté onions over medium-high heat. Season with salt, and let cook until onions are soft and lightly browned. Add garlic, ginger, turmeric, cumin, cinnamon, cloves, and cayenne, and let cook for a few more minutes until fragrant. Add chickpeas, tomatoes, and water. Season with salt and pepper. Reduce heat to medium and let simmer for 10 minutes. Mix in cilantro, brown sugar, and lemon juice and adjust seasoning to taste. Let cool and pulse in food processor until mixture comes together but is still slightly chunky.

To assemble the panini: Spread Tamarind-Mango Chutney on each bread slice and layer Spiced Chickpea Masala, Roasted Cauliflower Curry, and a few leaves of spinach in between slices. Brush the outsides of the panini with oil and press carefully on a hot panini press so that the filling does not come out the sides. Slice panini in half diagonally and serve immediately.

. . . .

Chloe's Tip: How to Cut a Mango

Mangoes have a large oblong pit so you cannot slice through the center. Place the mango upright on your cutting board and cut the flat sides off, running your knife along the pit, so that you have two oval pieces. Score the flesh of each piece, lengthwise and crosswise, cutting just to the skin. Push the scored flesh outward by pressing your fingers on the peel to turn the flesh inside out. Run the blade of a sharp paring knife between the inside of the mango peel and the scored mango flesh to cut off the diced sections.

. . . .

Chloe's Kitchen

Double Double Drive-Thru Burgers

SERVES 4

No guilty feelings about supersizing on this big bruiser! This is by far the best burger I've ever tasted and a whole lot better for you than anything found in a drive-through. Have it your way and top it with your favorite burger fixin's!

Make-Ahead Tip

Uncooked burger patties can be made in advance and kept frozen for up to 1 month or refrigerated for 3 to 4 days until ready to cook. The Special Sauce can be made in advance and kept refrigerated for 2 to 3 days.

BURGERS

1 8-ounce package tempeh, or 1 cup cooked brown rice

2 tablespoons olive oil

1 onion, finely chopped

2 cloves garlic, minced

1 15-ounce can lentils, rinsed and drained

1 cup walnuts, toasted

½ cup all-purpose flour, or gluten-free all-purpose flour

1 teaspoon dried basil

1 teaspoon sea salt

1 teaspoon freshly ground black pepper

3 tablespoons canola oil

SPECIAL SAUCE

⅔ cup soft tofu

1 clove garlic

1 tablespoon yellow or Dijon mustard

3 tablespoons ketchup

1 tablespoon agave

½ teaspoon salt

2 tablespoons pickle relish

1 tablespoon chopped fresh dill

8 burger buns, toasted, plus extra bottom halves for the middle layer

Optional toppings: Sliced tomato, sliced red onion, lettuce or other greens, pickle slices

To make the Burgers: Fill a large pot with enough water to reach the bottom of a steamer basket. Using a knife or your hands, break tempeh into 4 pieces and place in the basket.

(continued on page 105)

Double Double Drive-Thru Burgers (*cont.*)

Cover and steam for 20 minutes. Check the pot occasionally and add more water if necessary. Steaming the tempeh will remove its bitterness.

In the meantime, heat olive oil in a large nonstick skillet over medium-high heat, and sauté onions until soft and lightly browned. Add garlic and cook a few more minutes. Transfer to a food processor. Reserve skillet for later use.

Add steamed tempeh, lentils, walnuts, flour, basil, salt, and pepper to the onions in the food processor. Pulse until the walnut pieces are very fine and the mixture comes together. If necessary, transfer the mixture to a large bowl and mix with your hands. Adjust seasoning to taste. From the mixture into eight burger patties with the palms of your hands. The patties should be very thin if you are assembling your burger double-double style. For a restaurant-style burger, form a thicker patty.

Heat canola oil in reserved nonstick skillet over medium-high heat, and pan-fry patties in batches, adding more oil as needed. Flip the patties, and let cook until they are nicely browned on both sides. Remove patties from pan and drain on paper towels.

To make the Special Sauce: Combine tofu, garlic, mustard, ketchup, agave, and salt in a blender and process until smooth. Transfer to a small bowl and stir in relish and dill.

To serve: Layer the Burgers, Special Sauce, and other desired toppings on the buns. Make it double-double style by adding an extra bottom bun and burger in the middle, as pictured.

Falafel Sliders with Avocado Hummus

SERVES 4

Middle East meets California in these fun and flavorful Falafel Sliders. Jazzed up with fresh Avocado Hummus and a splash of creamy Tahini Sauce, these miniburgers are dressed to impress. If you want to ditch the bun, serve them over rice for a gluten-free Greek plate.

Make-Ahead Tip

The Falafel Sliders can be made in advance and frozen for up to 1 month or kept refrigerated for 3 to 4 days until ready to cook. The Tahini Sauce can be made in advance and kept refrigerated for 2 to 3 days.

FALAFEL SLIDERS

- 1 15-ounce can chickpeas, rinsed and drained, divided
- ½ red onion, finely chopped
- 2 cloves garlic, quartered
- 5 sun-dried tomatoes packed in oil, drained
- ½ cup packed fresh Italian parsley
- 1 teaspoon ground cumin
- 1 teaspoon ground coriander
- 1 teaspoon sea salt
- ½ cup garbanzo or other flour
- 2 tablespoons olive oil

AVOCADO HUMMUS

- ¼ cup chickpeas, reserved from sliders
- 1 avocado, pitted and peeled
- ⅓ cup packed fresh Italian parsley
- ¼ cup olive oil
- 1 clove garlic
- 1 tablespoon lemon juice
- ½ teaspoon sea salt
- ¼ teaspoon cayenne

TAHINI SAUCE

- ½ cup tahini
- ½ cup water
- 1 clove garlic
- 1 tablespoon lemon juice
- ½ teaspoon salt

- 14 slider buns or dinner rolls sliced in half, toasted
- 2 small tomatoes, thinly sliced

(continued on next page)

Falafel Sliders with Avocado Hummus (*cont.*)

To make the Falafel Sliders: Reserve ¼ cup chickpeas for the Avocado Hummus. Place remaining chickpeas, onions, garlic, tomatoes, parsley, cumin, coriander, salt, and flour in a food processor and pulse until combined, stopping frequently to scrape down sides. Using the palms of your hands, form mixture into 2-inch by ½-inch patties.

In a large nonstick skillet, heat oil over medium-high heat and pan-fry patties in batches, letting cook about 3 to 5 minutes on each side, until nicely browned. Do not crowd the pan. Remove from pan and drain on paper towels.

To make the Avocado Hummus: Combine ¼ cup chickpeas, avocado, parsley, oil, garlic, lemon juice, salt, and cayenne in food processor and puree. Adjust seasoning to taste.

To make the Tahini Sauce: Puree tahini, water, garlic, lemon juice, and salt until smooth.

To serve: Layer the Falafel Sliders, Avocado Hummus, Tahini Sauce, and sliced tomato on the buns.

LA-Style Chimichurri Tacos

SERVES 6

In Los Angeles, it's extremely popular to use nontraditional fillings for tacos. Angelenos love the anything-goes approach when it comes to taco combinations. I decided to get a little crazy with South American Chimichurri Sauce and the results were fantastic. Say adios *to lard and shredded pork and* hola *to these fresh, unique, and low-fat tacos.*

Make-Ahead Tip

All components of the tacos can be made in advance and kept refrigerated for 3 to 4 days. Reheat and assemble when ready to serve.

TOMATO RICE

2 tablespoons olive oil

1 onion, finely chopped

½ teaspoon sea salt

1 tomato, finely chopped

½ cup brown or white rice

1 cup vegetable broth

CHIMICHURRI SAUCE

1 cup fresh cilantro

½ cup fresh Italian parsley

½ cup olive oil

¼ cup lime juice

4 cloves garlic

2 tablespoons agave

½ teaspoon ground cumin

1 teaspoon sea salt

½ teaspoon freshly ground black pepper

TACO FILLING

2 tablespoons olive oil

8 ounces crimini mushrooms, trimmed and sliced

1 15-ounce can black beans, rinsed and drained

1 package 8-inch tortillas

Optional toppings: Sour Cream (page 254), chopped tomatoes, sliced onion, shredded lettuce, or diced avocado

(continued on page 111)

To make the Tomato Rice: In a medium saucepan, heat oil over medium-high heat and add onions and salt. Sauté onions until soft. Add tomato, rice, and broth and bring to a boil. Reduce heat to low and simmer, covered, until all broth is absorbed and rice is cooked. Turn off heat and let sit, covered, 15 minutes.

To make the Chimichurri Sauce: Blend cilantro, parsley, oil, lime juice, garlic, agave, cumin, salt, and pepper in a food processor until combined and herbs are very finely chopped.

To make the Taco Filling: In a large skillet, heat oil over medium-high heat and sauté mushrooms until they have released their juices. Add black beans and half of the Chimichurri Sauce and cook until heated through. Reserve the remaining half of the Chimichurri Sauce to spoon onto the taco, if desired.

To serve: Fill each tortilla with Tomato Rice, Taco Filling, extra Chimichurri Sauce, desired additional toppings, and a dollop of Sour Cream. Fold over and serve.

Moo Shu Vegetables
with Homemade Chinese Pancakes

SERVES 6 TO 8

There is nothing better than fresh hot pancakes. Oh, wait—except for fresh hot savory pancakes slathered in sweet hoisin sauce and filled with stir-fried veggies and tofu! There will be oohing and aahing at the table when you serve this Chinese-restaurant–style dish. Your guests will love the assembly-is-required fun of putting their own pancakes together.

For a shortcut, use flour tortillas instead of making pancakes.

VEGETABLES

1 14-ounce package extra-firm tofu, drained

4 tablespoons canola oil, divided

3 tablespoons soy sauce, divided

1 onion, thinly sliced

8 ounces mushrooms of choice, sliced

Sea salt

2 teaspoons grated fresh ginger

2 cloves garlic, minced

7 ounces cole slaw mix or shredded cabbage

1 cup shredded carrot

½ cup vegetable broth

2 scallions, trimmed and thinly sliced

SAUCE

¼ cup hoisin sauce

2 tablespoons soy sauce

CHINESE PANCAKES

2 cups all-purpose flour, plus extra for rolling

½ teaspoon sea salt

1 cup boiling water

Sesame oil, for brushing

To make the vegetables: Press the tofu according to directions on page 252. After pressing, cut tofu into thin rectangles. Heat 2 tablespoons oil in a large nonstick skillet over medium-high heat and add tofu. Drizzle 2 tablespoons soy sauce over the tofu. Flip tofu with a spatula, and let cook until both sides are nicely browned. Transfer to bowl.

(continued on next page)

Add remaining 2 tablespoons oil to the skillet and heat over medium-high heat. Add onions and mushrooms, and sauté until soft. Season with salt, add ginger and garlic, and let cook a few more minutes until fragrant. Add cole slaw mix, carrots, broth, and remaining 1 tablespoon soy sauce. Let cook, stirring frequently, until most of the liquid evaporates. Add tofu and scallions and adjust seasoning to taste. The flavor should be mild and light. Remove from heat.

To make the sauce: In a small serving bowl, whisk together hoisin sauce and soy sauce until combined.

To make the Chinese Pancakes: In a large bowl, whisk together flour and salt and add boiling water. Mix with a wooden spoon until dough is cool enough to mix with your hands. Knead for a few minutes on a lightly floured surface then let sit covered with a kitchen towel for 20 minutes.

Roll dough into a 16-inch log and cut it into 16 1-inch pieces. Flatten each piece of dough with the palm of your hand and roll out into a thin circle on a lightly floured surface. Each dough circle should be as thin as a tortilla and about 6 inches in diameter.

Heat a medium nonstick skillet or griddle over medium-high heat. Brush each dough circle with sesame oil on both sides. Cook the pancakes, one at a time, in the skillet. Once the pancake begins to bubble and brown on the bottom side, flip the pancake with a flat spatula and cook on the other side, about 30 seconds more. Remove from heat and stack cooked pancakes.

To serve: Serve Chinese Pancakes, vegetables, and sauce in separate serving bowls. Have your guests assemble their own Moo Shu by spreading the sauce on the Chinese Pancakes, topping them with the vegetables, and rolling them up.

Chloe's Tip: Keeping Pancakes and Crepes Hot

My friend, Nawal, from culinary school, taught me this ingenious trick to keep pancakes, crepes, or tortillas warm and fresh before you serve them. Stack the pancakes on a large, flat, heatproof plate. Fill a medium saucepan with a couple of inches of water and place on the stove over low heat. Put the plate of stacked pancakes on top of the saucepan; cover pancakes with a metal bowl. Pancakes can sit like this for a few hours, but be careful when lifting the bowl because everything will be hot.

Portobello Pesto Panini

Juicy portobello mushrooms, sweet caramelized onions, and tangy Artichoke Walnut Pesto, all pressed inside crusty ciabatta. Try these flavorful panini hot off the press and you'll never eat another cold sandwich again!

Make-Ahead Tip

Artichoke Walnut Pesto can be made in advance and kept frozen for up to 1 month or refrigerated for 2 to 3 days. Thaw and mix well before using.

4 tablespoons olive oil, divided, plus
   extra for brushing
1 large onion, thinly sliced
Sea salt
6 portobello mushrooms, stemmed and
   cut into ¼-inch slices

Freshly ground black pepper
Artichoke Walnut Pesto (page 15)
4 ciabatta rolls, halved, or 8 slices
   sandwich bread
1 large tomato, sliced
½ cup spinach or arugula

Preheat panini press to high.

In a large skillet, heat 2 tablespoons oil over medium heat. Add onions and let cook about 20 to 30 minutes, until tender and caramelized. Season with salt, and transfer to a bowl.

In the same skillet, heat remaining 2 tablespoons oil and sauté mushrooms over medium-high heat. Season with salt and pepper to taste and cook until mushrooms are lightly browned and the juices have evaporated.

To assemble the panini: Spread Artichoke Walnut Pesto on each bread slice and layer onions, mushrooms, tomatoes, and spinach in between slices. Brush the outsides of the panini with oil and press on a hot panini press until nice grill marks appear. Slice panini in half diagonally and serve immediately.

Rosemary Tomato Galette with Pine Nut Ricotta

SERVES 6

Think of this savory recipe as a French take on pizza. A galette (ga-LET) is a rustic French pastry tart that can be sweet or savory. My first experience with galette making was at Millennium restaurant in San Francisco when I was asked to make 250 galettes in one day for a prix fixe dinner that night. Luckily, I whipped them out like nobody's business and realized how easy they are to make. I assure you, after making only one galette—voila—you'll be a pro!

Make-Ahead Tip

The Pine Nut Ricotta can be made in advance and kept refrigerated for 2 to 3 days.

PINE NUT RICOTTA

1 small head garlic
¼ cup plus 1 tablespoon olive oil
Sea salt
Freshly ground black pepper

½ cup pine nuts, soaked overnight or boiled for 10 minutes, drained
1 tablespoon lemon juice

ROSEMARY TOMATO GALETTE

2½ cups all-purpose flour, or half all-purpose flour and half whole-wheat pastry flour, plus extra for rolling
1 tablespoon sugar
1 teaspoon salt
1 tablespoon chopped fresh rosemary

1 cup nonhydrogenated vegetable shortening or vegan margarine (if using margarine, omit salt)
½ cup ice-cold water, as needed
Olive oil for brushing
2 large tomatoes, heirloom, if available, thinly sliced

To make the Pine Nut Ricotta: Preheat the oven to 375 degrees.

Peel away the papery outer layers of the garlic head, but leave the individual garlic skins intact. Slice off the pointy end of the head of garlic, so that the tips of all cloves are exposed.

(continued on page 119)

Rosemary Tomato Galette with Pine Nut Ricotta (*cont.*)

Place the head of garlic on foil, cut-side up, and drizzle with 1 tablespoon oil and season with salt and pepper. Loosely fold up the ends of the foil pouch and pinch to seal. Roast for 30 to 40 minutes until the garlic cloves are fork tender. Remove from the oven and let cool. Once cooled, squeeze the head of garlic and the soft cloves will pop out. Set aside.

In a food processor, blend soaked nuts, roasted garlic, ¼ cup oil, lemon juice, ½ teaspoon salt, and ¼ teaspoon pepper. Scrape down the sides with a spatula frequently to make sure that all the ingredients are incorporated.

Remove mixture from the food processor, place in a medium bowl, and adjust seasoning to taste.

To make the Rosemary Tomato Galette: You can make the dough by hand or using a food processor.

By hand: In a medium bowl, whisk together flour, sugar, salt, and rosemary. Using a pastry cutter, cut shortening into flour until mixture has a crumbly consistency. Add ice water, 1 tablespoon at a time, and mix with a wooden spoon until dough just holds together. You may not need to use all of the water. Do not overwork.

Food processor: In a food processor, add flour, sugar, salt, and rosemary. Pulse until ingredients are combined. Add shortening and pulse until mixture has a crumbly consistency. Add ice water, 1 tablespoon at a time, and pulse until dough just holds together. You may not need to use all of the water. Do not overprocess.

Form the dough into a disc and wrap in plastic wrap. Refrigerate for 10 minutes.

Preheat the oven to 375 degrees. Line a large baking sheet with parchment paper.

Remove the dough from the refrigerator and unwrap it. Roll dough to ⅛-inch thickness between two layers of lightly floured parchment paper. Using a sharp knife, cut the dough into three circles using an 8-inch round baking pan or plate for a template. Refrigerate the rolled out discs for 10 minutes.

(continued on next page)

Rosemary Tomato Galette with Pine Nut Ricotta (*cont.*)

Remove discs from the refrigerator and brush the tops with oil. Fan tomatoes, overlapping, in a circular shape in the center of each disc, leaving a 1-inch border. Fold the 1-inch border of dough over the edges of the tomatoes and refrigerate for 15 minutes.

Transfer unbaked galettes to prepared baking sheet and brush with oil. Bake for 30 to 35 minutes until tomatoes look shriveled and crust is lightly browned. When the galettes come out of the oven, the tomatoes will be piping hot. Let the galettes cool for at least 5 minutes.

To serve: Cut galettes into quarters and top each slice with a dollop of Pine Nut Ricotta. For a fancy touch, pipe the ricotta onto each slice using a cake-decorating pastry bag and star tip. Serve warm.

Thai Chickpea Burgers with Sweet 'n' Spicy Sauce

SERVES 6

When I want something exotic and exciting but easy to whip up, I make these fusion-style burgers. I always keep a can of chickpeas (also known as garbanzo beans) on hand because they are loaded with protein and so convenient. Try these for a nice change of pace from your usual veggie burger.

Make-Ahead Tip

Uncooked Chickpea Patties can be made in advance and kept frozen for up to 1 month or refrigerated for 3 to 4 days until ready to cook. The Sweet 'n' Spicy Sauce can be made in advance and refrigerated for 3 to 4 days.

CHICKPEA PATTIES

1 15-ounce can chickpeas, rinsed and drained	¼ cup packed fresh cilantro
	½ cup bread crumbs
1 small onion, chopped	1 tablespoon lime juice
2 cloves garlic	1 teaspoon sea salt
1 teaspoon grated fresh ginger	2 tablespoons canola oil
½ small jalapeño or green chili, seeded and finely chopped	

SWEET 'N' SPICY SAUCE

1 6-ounce can tomato paste	1 teaspoon white or apple-cider vinegar
2 tablespoons olive oil	
2 tablespoons water	½ teaspoon crushed red pepper
3 tablespoons agave	¼ teaspoon sea salt

6 burger buns, lightly toasted	Sliced avocado

To make the Chickpea Patties: Place chickpeas, onions, garlic, ginger, jalapeño, cilantro, bread crumbs, lime juice, and salt in a food processor and pulse until just combined, stopping frequently to scrape down sides. Using the palms of your hands, form mixture into six burger patties.

(continued on next page)

Thai Chickpea Burgers with Sweet 'n' Spicy Sauce (*cont.*)

In a large nonstick skillet, heat oil over medium-high heat and pan-fry patties, letting them cook about 3 to 5 minutes on each side. Once patties are nicely browned, remove from heat and drain on paper towels.

To make the Sweet 'n' Spicy Sauce: In a blender, puree tomato paste, oil, water, agave, vinegar, red pepper, and salt. Adjust ingredients to taste.

To serve: Layer the Chickpea Patties, Sweet 'n' Spicy Sauce, and sliced avocado on the buns.

Oodles of Noodles

Avocado Pesto Pasta

SERVES 4 TO 6

Put a healthful California twist on a traditional Italian favorite and you've got Avocado Pesto Pasta. Adding avocado to pesto creates a rich and creamy texture without using cheese. Kids and adults often tell me this is the best pasta they've ever eaten!

1 pound linguine

1 bunch fresh basil, reserve some leaves
    for garnish

½ cup pine nuts

2 avocados, pitted and peeled

2 tablespoons lemon juice

3 cloves garlic

½ cup olive oil

Sea salt

Freshly ground black pepper

1 cup halved cherry tomatoes or sliced
    sun-dried tomatoes, optional

Bring a large pot of heavily salted water to a boil. Add linguine and cook according to package directions. Drain and set aside.

Meanwhile, make the pesto by combining basil, pine nuts, avocados, lemon juice, garlic, and oil in a food processor. Process until smooth. Season generously with salt and pepper.

Toss pasta with pesto. For an extra touch of color and flavor, top pasta with cherry or sun-dried tomatoes. Divide pasta among serving bowls and garnish each serving with a basil leaf.

Best-Ever Baked Macaroni and Cheese

SERVES 6

I love the sound of mac 'n' cheese. There's nothing like the sweet sound of suctioning noodles as you mix them with the cheesy sauce. Of course, the taste is even better. Mmmm, brings me back to my childhood when mac 'n' cheese gooey goodness was a way of life!

The consistency of this sauce is enhanced by a roux, a mixture of fat and flour that is cooked over low heat until it is bubbling and the raw starchy taste has cooked out. Roux is used to thicken soups, stews, and sauces.

Make-Ahead Tip
Unbaked macaroni and cheese can be refrigerated for 2 to 3 days until ready to bake.

1 pound elbow macaroni	2 tablespoons tomato paste
¼ cup vegan margarine	2 teaspoons sea salt
⅓ cup all-purpose flour, or gluten-free all-purpose flour	1 teaspoon garlic powder
	1 tablespoon lemon juice
3 cups soy, almond, or rice milk	1 tablespoon agave
½ cup nutritional yeast flakes	2 tablespoons seasoned bread crumbs

Preheat the oven to 350 degrees. Lightly grease a 9 x 13-inch pan.

Bring a large pot of heavily salted water to a boil. Add macaroni and cook according to package directions. Drain and return to pot.

Meanwhile, in a medium saucepan, make a *roux* by whisking the margarine and flour over medium heat for a few minutes until it forms a paste. Add nondairy milk, nutritional yeast, tomato paste, salt, and garlic powder to the saucepan and bring to a boil, whisking frequently. Reduce heat to low and let simmer until the sauce thickens. Adjust seasoning to taste and stir in lemon juice and agave. Toss noodles with the sauce and transfer to the prepared pan. Sprinkle bread crumbs on top of the pasta and bake for 30 minutes, or until the top is lightly browned and crisp. Remove from oven and let rest for 5 minutes before serving.

Chinese Takeout Chow Mein

This recipe is quick and easy just like takeout but much more healthful. Your friends and family will be totally amazed when they find out you made it yourself.

8 ounces spaghetti or Asian noodles

2 cups broccoli florets

½ cup frozen peas

¼ cup hoisin sauce

¼ cup vegetable broth

3 tablespoons soy sauce

2 teaspoons chili-garlic sauce

2 tablespoons canola oil

1 onion, thinly sliced

8 ounces mushrooms of choice, sliced

1 carrot, peeled and cut into matchsticks

4 scallions, trimmed and thinly sliced

3 cloves garlic, minced

1 teaspoon ground ginger

1 teaspoon ground coriander

1 cup bean sprouts

Sea salt

Bring a large pot of heavily salted water to a boil. Add spaghetti and cook according to package directions. Add broccoli to the pot for the last 5 minutes and cook until broccoli is fork tender. Add peas to the boiling pasta right before draining. Drain and set aside.

Meanwhile, make the sauce by mixing hoisin sauce, broth, soy sauce, and chili-garlic sauce in a small bowl. Set aside.

In a large skillet, heat oil over medium-high heat and sauté onions, mushrooms, and carrot until vegetables are soft and lightly browned. Add scallions, garlic, ginger, and coriander; let cook a few more minutes until fragrant.

Add cooked spaghetti, broccoli, and peas and let cook a few minutes more. Add bean sprouts and sauce. Let cook, stirring constantly, until pasta is heated through and coated with sauce. Add salt if needed and serve immediately.

(continued on next page)

Chloe's Tip: Takeout Box

Drop by your local Chinese restaurant and ask for a takeout container to plate your noodles. I did this once for my friends and they were raving that it was the best takeout they have ever had. Naturally, I couldn't keep a straight face and the jig was up!

Chloe's Kitchen

Orecchiette in No-Cook Spinach Sauce

SERVES 4 TO 6

There's nothing like a good no-cook pasta sauce for the days when you need to whip something up without a lot of fuss. Simply toss your hot pasta with lima beans, green beans, and tangy garlic spinach sauce for a gorgeous green meal in a hurry. This pasta is called orecchiette, which means "little ear," because of its cupped shape. It is one of my favorites, but feel free to use any other shape you have on hand. Leftovers make a delicious cold pasta salad.

1 pound orecchiette

4 ounces fresh or frozen green beans, ends trimmed, cut into 1-inch pieces

10 ounces frozen lima beans, thawed

5 ounces baby spinach

3 cloves garlic

¼ cup olive oil

¼ cup water

1 tablespoon lemon juice

1 teaspoon sea salt

½ teaspoon freshly ground black pepper

Bring a large pot of heavily salted water to a boil. Add orecchiette and cook according to package directions. With about 5 minutes remaining, add green beans and lima beans to boiling pasta water and let cook until they are fork tender and pasta is cooked. Drain and set aside.

Meanwhile, make the sauce by combining spinach, garlic, oil, water, lemon juice, salt, and pepper in a food processor. Process until smooth.

In a large serving bowl, toss pasta with green beans, lima beans, and sauce. Adjust seasoning to taste and serve. Any leftovers can be served warm or cold the next day for a delicious lunch.

Drunken Noodles
in Cashew-Shiitake Broth

SERVES 4 TO 6

Dive in! This Asian noodle soup will nourish your body and warm your soul. Udon noodles are big, fat, toothsome Japanese wheat flour noodles—they taste crazy delicious when swimming in savory cashew-shiitake broth.

6 ounces dried udon noodles, or 12 ounces cooked

2 tablespoons olive oil

8 ounces shiitake mushrooms, stemmed and sliced

3 scallions, trimmed and thinly sliced

4 cloves garlic, minced

1 tablespoon grated fresh ginger

¼ jalapeño pepper, seeded and finely chopped

Pinch cayenne

5 cups vegetable broth

1 tablespoon rice vinegar

1 tablespoon toasted sesame oil

Sea salt

¼ cup cashews, toasted and roughly chopped

Chopped fresh cilantro, for garnish

If you are using dried noodles, bring a large pot of heavily salted water to a boil. Add udon noodles and cook according to package directions. Drain and set aside.

Meanwhile, heat oil in a large pot over medium-high heat. Add mushrooms and scallions and let cook until mushrooms are soft and lightly browned. Add garlic, ginger, jalapeño, and cayenne; let cook a few more minutes.

Add broth and bring to a boil. Add noodles, reduce heat to low, and simmer, covered, for 10 minutes. Turn off heat and stir in vinegar and sesame oil. Season to taste with salt and garnish with cashews and cilantro. Serve immediately.

Fettuccine Alfredo

SERVES 4 TO 6

There is something oh-so-comforting about slurping up hot fettuccine coated in a decadent cream sauce. But hold the cream! This dairy-free vegan version is every bit as rich and satisfying, with only half the fat. Who says you can't have it all? Made with a heavenly garlic-infused cashew or almond cream sauce and flecked with fresh parsley, this Fettuccine Alfredo is even tastier than the real deal. It also leaves you feeling light and energized, without a pasta hangover.

1 pound fettuccine
2 tablespoons olive oil
1 large onion, chopped
3 cloves garlic, minced
1 cup raw cashews or blanched
    almonds*
2 cups water

2 teaspoons white miso paste,
    optional
1 tablespoon lemon juice
1 teaspoon sea salt
¼ teaspoon freshly ground black
    pepper
Chopped fresh Italian parsley, for
    garnish

Bring a large pot of heavily salted water to a boil. Add fettuccine and cook according to package directions. Drain and return to pot.

Meanwhile, heat oil in a medium skillet over medium-high heat. Add onions and let cook until soft. Add garlic and let cook a few more minutes. Remove from heat.

In a blender, combine onions and garlic, cashews, water, miso paste if desired, lemon juice, salt, and pepper. Process on high until very smooth, about 2 minutes.

Toss hot pasta with sauce until noodles are evenly coated. Adjust seasoning to taste. If sauce gets too thick, add a little water, 1 tablespoon at a time. Garnish with parsley and serve.

*If you are not using a high-powered blender, such as a Vitamix, soak cashews or almonds overnight or boil for 10 minutes and drain. This will soften them and ensure a silky smooth cream.

Ooh-La-La Lasagna

SERVES 6 TO 8

With a last name like Coscarelli, I know my lasagna. So trust me when I say this is the best vegan lasagna you will ever make!

Make-Ahead Tip
Unbaked lasagna can be assembled and refrigerated for 2 to 3 days until ready to bake.

GARDEN RICOTTA

2 tablespoons olive oil

1 onion, chopped

3 cloves garlic

1 14-ounce package extra-firm tofu, drained

2 tablespoons lemon juice

1½ teaspoons sea salt

1½ teaspoons freshly ground black pepper

1 tablespoon white miso paste

3 cups fresh basil

SAUCE

2 tablespoons olive oil

8 ounces crimini mushrooms, sliced

1 24-ounce jar marinara sauce, purchased or prepared following recipe on page 255

1 pound no-boil lasagna noodles

¼ cup soy, almond, or rice milk

1 tablespoon brown sugar or maple syrup

Sea salt

Freshly ground black pepper

5 ounces baby spinach

Preheat the oven to 375 degrees. Lightly grease a 9 x 13-inch pan.

To make the Garden Ricotta: In a large skillet, heat oil over medium heat and sauté onions until soft. Remove from heat.

In the food processor, combine onions, garlic, tofu, lemon juice, salt, pepper, and miso paste. Pulse until mixture is almost smooth but still has some texture. Add basil and pulse a few more times to incorporate the basil. Adjust seasoning to taste.

To make the sauce: Heat oil over medium-high heat in a large skillet, and sauté mushrooms until soft. Add marinara sauce, nondairy milk, and brown sugar and heat through. The nondairy milk and brown sugar will soften the acidity of the tomatoes. Add salt and pepper to taste.

To assemble and bake the lasagna: Spread a thin layer of sauce on the bottom of the prepared pan. Arrange 4 lasagna noodles across the pan. Spread half of the Garden Ricotta over the noodles. Layer half of the spinach over the Garden Ricotta. Arrange 4 more noodles on top. Spread another layer of sauce over the noodles, then arrange 4 more noodles on top. Top with another layer of sauce, the remaining Garden Ricotta, the remaining spinach, and 4 more noodles. Top with remaining sauce. You may have some noodles left over.

Cover the baking pan with foil and bake for 45 minutes, or until noodles are cooked and sauce is hot and bubbling. Remove from oven and let rest for 5 minutes before serving.

Pasta Italiano

SERVES 4 TO 6

This is my version of pasta and beans: fusilli in a creamy white bean sauce with asparagus tips and fresh cherry tomatoes. In Italy, eating pasta and beans with someone signifies close friendship. My dear friend, Danielle, who lives in Italy, says that Italians even use this dish to describe how close they are with somebody. For example, "I had fun with her, but it's not like we would eat pasta and beans together." Needless to say, Danielle and I have eaten pasta and beans together many times. Invite your best pals for this one and pile your plates high!

1 pound fusilli

1 bunch asparagus, ends trimmed, cut into 1-inch pieces

2 15-ounce cans cannellini or other white beans, rinsed and drained, divided into two equal portions

1 cup soy, almond, or rice milk

¼ cup olive oil

3 cloves garlic

1 tablespoon lemon juice

1 teaspoon dried thyme

1½ teaspoons sea salt

½ teaspoon freshly ground black pepper

½ teaspoon crushed red pepper

1 cup cherry tomatoes, halved lengthwise

In a large pot, cook fusilli in heavily salted water for 8 minutes. Add asparagus to boiling pasta water and let cook for an additional 5 minutes, or until asparagus is fork tender and pasta is cooked. Drain and return to pot.

Meanwhile, make the sauce by combining 1 can of white beans, nondairy milk, oil, garlic, lemon juice, thyme, salt, and pepper in a food processor. Process until smooth.

Toss hot pasta and asparagus with the sauce, remaining can of white beans, red pepper, and tomatoes. Adjust seasoning to taste and serve. If you are not serving the pasta immediately, you may need to add a little more nondairy milk when you reheat it.

Chloe's Kitchen

Chloe's Tip: Asparagus Tip

Keep the grocery store rubber bands on the bunch of asparagus while you trim the ends, so that they stay put on your cutting board.

Peanutty Perfection Noodles

This is my favorite recipe in the book. Super creamy, slightly sweet, and subtly spicy—noodle nirvana.

1 pound brown rice noodles

1 cup coconut milk

½ cup water

¼ cup maple syrup

¼ cup soy sauce

½ cup peanut butter, chunky or creamy

1 tablespoon chili-garlic sauce

1 teaspoon grated fresh ginger

3 cloves garlic, minced

2 tablespoons lime juice

1 tablespoon toasted sesame oil

3 scallions, trimmed and thinly sliced

2 carrots, peeled and shredded

½ cup peanuts, roughly chopped, for garnish

2 tablespoons roughly chopped fresh cilantro, for garnish

Bring a large pot of heavily salted water to a boil. Add brown rice noodles and cook according to package directions. Drain, rinse with cold water, and drain again. Return noodles to pot.

Meanwhile, make the sauce by combining coconut milk, water, maple syrup, soy sauce, peanut butter, chili-garlic sauce, ginger, and garlic in a medium saucepan. Let cook over medium heat, whisking frequently, until sauce comes together and thickens. Remove from heat and mix in lime juice and sesame oil.

Toss hot noodles with the sauce, scallions, and carrots. Garnish with peanuts and cilantro and serve. Any leftovers can be served warm or cold the next day for a delicious lunch.

Penne alla Vodka with the Best Garlic Bread in the World

SERVES 4 TO 6

Cooking a romantic dinner for two? Trying to impress the in-laws? This dish never fails. Just watch! Your guests will go nuts for this restaurant-style pasta in tomato cream sauce. P.S. Yes, this garlic bread really is the best in the world. Cheese hounds and butter-loving omnivores scarf it down hand over fist!

1 pound penne

2 tablespoons olive oil

3 cloves garlic, minced

1 28-ounce can crushed tomatoes

½ cup chopped fresh basil, plus extra for chiffonade garnish, see Tip (page 77)

Sea salt

Freshly ground black pepper

¼ cup vodka

¼ cup raw cashews*

1 cup water

Bring a large pot of heavily salted water to a boil. Add penne and cook according to package directions. Drain and return to pot.

Meanwhile, heat oil in a large saucepan over medium-high heat. Add garlic and cook about 1 minute. Stir in crushed tomatoes and basil. Season with salt and pepper. Cook over medium heat for 10 minutes, stirring occasionally. Stir in vodka and cook 10 more minutes, stirring occasionally.

In the meantime, combine cashews and water in a blender. Process on high until very smooth, about 2 minutes. Stir cashew cream into the tomato sauce and turn off heat. Adjust seasoning to taste and toss with hot pasta. Garnish with basil and serve immediately.

*If you are not using a high-powered blender, such as a Vitamix, soak cashews overnight or boil cashews for 10 minutes and drain. This will soften the cashews and ensure a silky smooth cream.

(continued on next page)

Penne alla Vodka with the Best Garlic Bread in the World (*cont.*)

THE BEST GARLIC BREAD IN THE WORLD

½ cup vegan margarine

¼ cup nutritional yeast

6 cloves garlic, minced

1 baguette

Dried or fresh parsley for garnish

Preheat the oven to broil.

Combine margarine, nutritional yeast, and garlic in a small microwave-safe bowl or saucepan. Heat in the microwave or in a small saucepan over low heat until the margarine is melted. Stir until combined.

Slice the baguette in half horizontally and place each half, cut side up, on a baking sheet. Spread the garlic mixture over each half. You may not need to use all of the garlic mixture. You can refrigerate or freeze any leftover garlic mixture for another use. Sprinkle parsley over each half and broil for about a minute or two, checking very frequently until lightly browned. Keep your eyes on the garlic bread, it can burn very quickly!

Chloe's Kitchen

Spaghetti Bolognese

SERVES 4 TO 6

This meatless mushroom Bolognese sauce is extremely hearty, high in protein, and fit for a very big appetite. My vegetarian Italian dad was hesitant to eat it at first because he didn't believe it was vegetarian when he tasted it. Trust me, it is, so eat up!

1 pound spaghetti

1 cup walnuts

8 ounces crimini mushrooms, trimmed and sliced

1 15-ounce can pinto or kidney beans, rinsed, drained, and patted dry

½ cup all-purpose flour, or gluten-free all-purpose flour

1 teaspoon dried basil

1 teaspoon sea salt

1 teaspoon ground black pepper

2 tablespoons olive oil

1 24-ounce jar marinara sauce, purchased or prepared following recipe on page 255

¼ cup soy, almond, or rice milk

1 tablespoon brown sugar or maple syrup

Chopped fresh basil for garnish, optional

Bring a large pot of heavily salted water to a boil. Add spaghetti and cook according to package directions. Drain and set aside.

Meanwhile, make the sauce by processing walnuts in a food processor until a fine crumbly meal forms. Add mushrooms and pulse about 15 times until mushrooms are finely chopped. Add beans, flour, basil, salt, and pepper and pulse about 10 more times. Do not overprocess; it should be crumbly and chunky.

Heat oil in a large nonstick skillet over medium-high heat. Transfer mushroom mixture to the pan and let cook, turning frequently with a spatula, until the mixture is evenly browned, about 10 to 15 minutes. Add marinara sauce, nondairy milk, and brown sugar and stir until heated through. The nondairy milk and brown sugar will soften the acidity of the tomatoes.

Top hot pasta with sauce, garnish with basil, and serve.

Straw and Hay Pasta

SERVES 4 TO 6

Straw and hay pasta, or Paglio e Fieno *in Italian, gets its name from the white and green linguine noodles that look like sticks of straw and hay. Tossed in a light and creamy sauce with juicy shiitake mushrooms and sun-dried tomatoes, these noodles make for a beautiful presentation. Who knew straw and hay could taste so good?*

8 ounces linguine

8 ounces spinach linguine

1 cup frozen peas

2 tablespoons olive oil

6 ounces shiitake mushrooms, stemmed
   and thinly sliced

Sea salt

Freshly ground black pepper

2 cups soy, almond, or rice milk

1 cup water

¼ cup cornstarch or arrowroot

2 tablespoons tahini

1 tablespoon soy sauce

3 cloves garlic

1 teaspoon onion powder

10 sun-dried tomatoes packed in oil,
   drained and chopped

Bring a large pot of heavily salted water to a boil. Add linguine and cook according to package directions. Add frozen peas to the boiling pasta right before draining. Drain and return to pot.

Meanwhile, heat oil in a large skillet over medium-high heat. Sauté mushrooms until soft and lightly browned. Season with salt and pepper to taste.

While mushrooms are cooking, prepare the sauce. Combine nondairy milk, water, cornstarch, tahini, soy sauce, garlic, onion powder, and 1¾ teaspoons salt in a blender. Blend until smooth. Transfer sauce to a medium saucepan and let cook over medium heat, whisking frequently, until thick (about 5 to 10 minutes).

Toss hot pasta and peas with mushrooms, sun-dried tomatoes, and sauce. Serve immediately.

Stuffed Shells with Arrabbiata Sauce

SERVES 4 TO 6

I love these jumbo shells stuffed with cheesy basil ricotta baked in spicy garlic tomato sauce. The Garden Ricotta is so flavorful that it can even stand alone as a great dip.

For a shortcut, buy a jar of Arrabbiata sauce.

Make-Ahead Tip

Unbaked stuffed shells can be refrigerated for 2 to 3 days until ready to bake.

1 pound jumbo shells
Garden Ricotta (page 136)

ARRABBIATA SAUCE

2 tablespoons olive oil
4 garlic cloves, minced
2 teaspoons Italian seasoning
½ teaspoon crushed red pepper
½ teaspoon sea salt
½ teaspoon freshly ground black pepper
1 28-ounce can crushed tomatoes
¼ cup soy, almond, or rice milk
1 tablespoon brown sugar or maple syrup

Preheat the oven to 375 degrees. Lightly grease a 9 x 13-inch pan.

Bring a large pot of heavily salted water to a boil. Add shells and cook according to package directions until just tender. Do not overcook because they will cook further in the oven. Drain the shells and let cool slightly.

To make the Arrabbiata Sauce: In a large saucepan, heat oil over medium heat and cook garlic, Italian seasoning, red pepper, salt, and pepper for 1 to 2 minutes. Add crushed tomatoes, and bring to a boil. Reduce heat to low and simmer, uncovered, for 15 minutes, or until the sauce thickens. Remove from heat and stir in nondairy milk and brown sugar, which will soften the acidity of the tomatoes. Adjust seasoning to taste.

(continued on next page)

Stuffed Shells with Arrabbiata Sauce (*cont.*)

To assemble the Shells: Stuff each shell with the Garden Ricotta. Pour some Arrabbiata Sauce into the prepared pan so that it lightly covers the bottom. Place the stuffed shells in the pan, then spoon some more sauce on top of the shells. Cover the shells with foil and bake for about 15 minutes. Remove the foil and continue baking until the shells are lightly browned and the Garden Ricotta is heated through, about 15 more minutes. Remove from oven. Top the shells with more Arrabbiata Sauce, if desired, and serve.

Sweet Potato Gnocchi with Sage Butter

SERVES 4 TO 6

Gnocchi (pronounced NYO-kee) are soft little pillows of potato heaven that pretty much put regular noodles to shame. I like to make the dough with sweet potatoes and pan-fry the gnocchi with a touch of vegan butter and fresh sage leaves. You get extra points if they make it to the plate before going into your mouth!

Make-Ahead Tip

Uncooked gnocchi can be made in advance and kept frozen for up to 1 month or refrigerated for 3 to 4 days until ready to boil.

2 large red-skinned sweet potatoes (about 2 pounds)

1 teaspoon sea salt

½ teaspoon ground nutmeg

¼ teaspoon freshly ground black pepper, plus extra for serving

2½ to 3½ cups all-purpose flour, plus extra for rolling

½ cup vegan margarine

½ cup fresh sage leaves

Preheat the oven to 425 degrees.

Pierce sweet potatoes with a fork, place in a baking pan, and bake until fully cooked, about 45 to 60 minutes. Remove from oven and let sit until cool enough to handle.

Using a sharp knife, cut the potatoes in half lengthwise. Using a large spoon, scoop the flesh out of each sweet potato into a medium bowl. Thoroughly mash the sweet potatoes while they are still warm, then set aside or refrigerate to cool completely.

Add salt, nutmeg, and pepper to the sweet potatoes. Add flour, ½ cup at a time, mixing well with a spoon to combine. Once a soft, slightly sticky, dough has formed, divide it into six portions. Generously flour the work surface and your hands. Roll each portion of dough

(continued on next page)

into ropes about ½ inch in diameter. Each rope will be approximately 7 to 9 inches long. Dip a sharp knife in flour and cut each rope into 1-inch long pillows. If desired, roll each pillow on fork tines to make decorative ridges.

Fill a medium saucepan with heavily salted water and bring it to a boil. In the meantime, heat margarine and sage in a large nonstick skillet until the margarine begins to bubble.

When the water is boiling, reduce heat to a gentle simmer and gently drop in the gnocchi, about 20 at a time. The gnocchi will float to the surface in about 4 minutes. Continue to cook about 30 seconds more. Using a slotted spoon, immediately transfer the gnocchi to the skillet of butter sauce. Let cook, turning frequently, for 1 to 2 minutes. You will have to do this in several batches, until all the gnocchi are cooked. Serve immediately, topped with additional freshly ground black pepper.

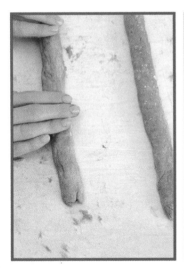  

Wild Mushroom Stroganoff Fettuccine

SERVES 4 TO 6

My mom and I have always loved sitting down to big hearty lunches together. She would often pick me up from school at lunchtime to eat a hot home-cooked meal, then drop me off, well-fed and raring to learn more! Sometimes we laugh because we eat lunch the way most people eat dinner, but it's just too hard for us to wait. Try this creamy mushroom pasta (lunch, dinner, whenever) and you'll never go back to PB&J sandwiches again!

1 pound fettuccine
2 tablespoons olive oil
1 yellow onion, chopped
8 ounces crimini mushrooms, trimmed and sliced
Sea salt
Freshly ground black pepper
3 garlic cloves, minced
3 tablespoons vegan margarine
3 tablespoons all-purpose flour, or gluten-free all-purpose flour

1 to 2 ounces dried porcini mushrooms, soaked in boiling water for 5 minutes and drained
3 cups soy, almond, or rice milk
¼ cup tomato paste
¼ cup white wine
½ teaspoon dried parsley
½ teaspoon dried thyme
½ cup chopped fresh chives, plus extra for garnish

Bring a large pot of heavily salted water to a boil. Add fettuccine and cook according to package directions. Drain and return to pot.

Meanwhile, heat oil in a large deep-sided skillet over medium-high heat. Add onions and crimini mushrooms and let cook until soft and lightly browned. Season generously with salt and pepper. Add garlic and let cook a few more minutes.

Push mushrooms and onions to the side of the skillet and reduce heat to medium. Add margarine and flour and whisk together to form a roux. Let cook a few minutes until it forms a paste.

Add porcini mushrooms, nondairy milk, tomato paste, wine, parsley, thyme, and chives, and mix together with the onion and mushroom mixture. Bring to a boil, then reduce heat to low and simmer, covered, for 15 minutes, or until sauce thickens. Adjust seasoning to taste and toss with hot pasta. Garnish with chives and serve immediately.

The Main Event

Barley Bliss Casserole

SERVES 8

*Barley is a high-fiber whole grain with a chewy, nutty texture. This creamy tomato barley dish is chock full of mushrooms, red beans, green peppers, and onions for the ultimate hearty casserole experience. If you're like me, you'll **barley** be able to stop eating it.*

2 tablespoons olive oil

1 large onion, finely chopped

1 green pepper, seeded and diced

8 ounces baby bella or crimini
   mushrooms, trimmed and sliced

2 teaspoons garlic powder

2 teaspoons dried thyme

2 teaspoons sea salt

½ teaspoon freshly ground black pepper

1 14-ounce can diced tomatoes,
   undrained

1 15-ounce can red kidney beans,
   rinsed and drained

1½ cups pearled barley

½ cup nutritional yeast flakes

2½ cups soy, almond, or rice milk

2 cups water

Preheat the oven to 350 degrees.

In a large skillet, heat olive oil over medium heat and sauté onions, green peppers, and mushrooms until soft and lightly browned. Add garlic powder, thyme, salt, and pepper and let cook a few more minutes.

Transfer vegetables to a 9 x 13-inch pan. Gently stir in tomatoes, beans, barley, nutritional yeast, nondairy milk, and water. The pan will be very full.

Cover pan with foil and carefully place in the oven. Let cook for 1 hour and 15 minutes, and then remove the foil. Let bake, uncovered, stirring occasionally with a wooden spoon, for 20 to 30 minutes more, or until barley is cooked and most of the liquid is absorbed. Remove from oven and let rest for 5 minutes before serving.

Caribbean Vegetables with Coconut Rice and Plantains

SERVES 4

For a little retreat from the ordinary, take a trip to the Caribbean with a big bowl of jerk-seasoned broccoli and sweet potatoes served with Cumin-Lime Black Beans, caramelized plantains, and sticky Coconut Rice.

COCONUT RICE

1½ cups jasmine or long-grain white rice

1 14-ounce can coconut milk

1 cup water

1 teaspoon sea salt

CARIBBEAN VEGETABLES

1 large red-skinned sweet potato, peeled and cut into ½-inch pieces

2 to 3 cups broccoli florets

Sea salt

1½ teaspoons jerk spice seasoning or a mixture of 1 teaspoon paprika, ¼ teaspoon ground cinnamon, ¼ teaspoon dried thyme leaves, and 1 or 2 pinches cayenne

CUMIN-LIME BLACK BEANS

1 15-ounce can black beans, rinsed and drained, divided

½ cup vegetable broth

2 cloves garlic

1 teaspoon ground cumin

2 teaspoons lime juice

Sea salt

PLANTAINS

2 tablespoons canola oil

1 large ripe plantain, peeled and cut into ¼-inch slices on the diagonal, see Tip (page 160)

Sea salt

(continued on next page)

Carribbean Vegetables with Coconut Rice and Plantains (*cont.*)

To make the Coconut Rice: In a medium saucepan, combine rice, coconut milk, water, and salt. Bring to a boil. Reduce heat to low and simmer, covered, until rice is cooked and liquid is absorbed. Remove from heat and let the rice sit and steam, covered, for 10 to 15 minutes.

To make the Caribbean Vegetables: In a medium saucepan with a steamer basket, steam sweet potatoes and broccoli for 20 minutes, or until all vegetables are fork tender. Season vegetables with salt and spice mix. Set aside.

To make the Cumin-Lime Black Beans: While the rice is cooking and the vegetables are steaming, make the bean puree by combining ½ can beans, broth, and garlic in a food processor. Puree until smooth.

In a medium saucepan, combine bean puree, remaining ½ can beans, cumin, and lime juice, and heat over medium heat. Season with salt to taste and cook until heated through.

To make the plantains: Heat oil in a large nonstick skillet over medium-high heat. Once oil is hot, add plantains and lightly season with salt. Let cook a few minutes on each side until nicely browned with crispy edges.

To serve: Serve buffet style or plate each serving with a little of each component.

. . . .

Chloe's Tip:

The plantain, which is related to the banana, is popular in tropical cuisines. It is not eaten raw like the banana, but instead cooked to bring out its sweet flavor. As the plantain ripens, it will go from green to yellow to black. For this dish, use the plantain when it is yellow with many black spots. Plantains can take up to 2 weeks to ripen so buy them well before you need them and keep them on your kitchen counter to ripen. To peel the plantain, cut off the tips with a sharp knife. Make 2 lengthwise slits on either side of the plantain and peel back the skin with your hands.

. . . .

Chloe's Kitchen

Country Meatloaf and Golden Gravy with Orange-Scented Cranberry Sauce

SERVES 8

Comfort food heaven right here! The savory aroma, reminiscent of winter holidays, will fill your kitchen as this delicious and hearty meatloaf bakes. Smother it in Golden Gravy and serve it with Orange-Scented Cranberry Sauce, Guilt-Free Garlic Mashed Potatoes (page 79), Maple-Roasted Brussels Sprouts with Toasted Hazelnuts (page 81), and Coconut Mashed Yams with Currants (page 73) for the whole holiday shebang. Consider yourself lucky if you have leftovers because it tastes even better the next day.

Note that the recipe can be halved to serve 4 people. If halving, bake in an 8- x 4- x 3-inch loaf pan for 30 minutes covered; then 15 more minutes uncovered.

Make-Ahead Tip

Unbaked meatloaf can be refrigerated for 2 to 3 days in advance until ready to bake. Cranberry sauce and gravy can also be made in advance and kept refrigerated for 2 to 3 days.

COUNTRY MEATLOAF

2 8-ounce packages tempeh

4 tablespoons olive oil, plus extra for brushing

2 large onions, finely chopped

2 large carrots, peeled and finely chopped

2 cups finely chopped celery

8 cloves garlic, minced

2 tablespoons fresh thyme leaves

2 teaspoons dried basil

2 teaspoons dried parsley

½ cup soy sauce

½ cup vegetable broth

1 cup cooked brown rice, warm

½ cup bread crumbs

Sea salt

Freshly ground black pepper

GOLDEN GRAVY

2 tablespoons canola oil

1 large onion, roughly chopped

¼ cup nutritional yeast flakes

½ cup all-purpose flour, or gluten-free all-purpose flour

2 cups water

3 tablespoons soy sauce

1 teaspoon dried thyme

1 teaspoon garlic powder

Sea salt

Freshly ground black pepper

(continued on page 163)

Country Meatloaf and Golden Gravy with Orange-Scented Cranberry Sauce (*cont.*)

8 ounces cranberries, fresh or frozen, about 2½ cups

½ cup maple syrup, plus extra to taste

¼ cup freshly squeezed orange juice, from about 1 orange

1 tablespoon orange zest, from about 1 orange

½ teaspoon ground cinnamon

¼ teaspoon ground ginger

Pinch salt

1 teaspoon pure vanilla extract

To make the Country Meatloaf: Preheat the oven to 350 degrees. Brush a 10- x 5- x 3-inch loaf pan with oil.

Fill a large pot with enough water to reach the bottom of a steamer basket. Using a knife or your hands, break each 8 ounces of tempeh into 4 pieces and place in the basket. Cover and steam for 20 minutes. Check the pot occasionally and add more water if necessary. Steaming the tempeh will remove its bitterness.

In the meantime, heat oil over medium-high heat in a large skillet and sauté onions, carrots, and celery until soft, about 20 minutes. If vegetables begin to stick, add a little bit of water to the skillet. Stir in garlic, thyme, basil, and parsley. Let cook a few more minutes. Crumble the steamed tempeh into the skillet and add soy sauce. Stir until tempeh is evenly coated with soy sauce and nicely browned.

Deglaze the pan of vegetables and tempeh by adding broth and scraping up the browned bits (known as *fond*) with your spoon or spatula. This will add a nice rich flavor to your meatloaf. Transfer the mixture to a large bowl.

Add warm brown rice and bread crumbs to the bowl and mix thoroughly with a large spoon. The more you mix it and mash it, the better it will hold together when you bake it. Season with pepper to taste, and add salt if needed.

Transfer the mixture into the prepared loaf pan and pack it down using the back of a spoon. It is important to pack it firmly so that it binds together while baking. Cover the top of the loaf pan with foil.

(*continued on next page*)

Country Meatloaf and Golden Gravy with Orange-Scented Cranberry Sauce (*cont.*)

Bake for 45 minutes, covered, then remove foil, and bake for an additional 15 minutes. Remove from oven and let rest for 5 minutes before unmolding. Run a knife around the edges of the cooked meatloaf to loosen, then flip onto a tray or plate to unmold. Slice and serve immediately.

To make the Golden Gravy: In a medium saucepan, heat oil over medium-high heat and sauté onions until soft. Add nutritional yeast and flour, and stir for about 1 minute. The mixture will be dry. Add water, soy sauce, thyme, and garlic powder. Continue to cook, whisking continuously, until mixture is very thick. Transfer gravy to a blender and puree until smooth. Adjust seasonings and add salt and pepper to taste.

To make the Orange-Scented Cranberry Sauce: In a medium saucepan, stir together cranberries, maple syrup, orange juice and zest, cinnamon, ginger, and salt. Bring to a boil then reduce heat to simmer. Let cook, stirring frequently, until cranberries pop and turn to cranberry sauce, about 15 minutes. Remove from heat, mix in vanilla, and add more maple syrup to taste.

Eggplant Timbales

SERVES 4

For my final exam in culinary school at The Natural Gourmet Institute in New York City, I worked with a team of six other classmates to plan and cook a three-course prix fixe dinner for one hundred guests. The event was open to the public, and we worked for three months to prepare for the big night. The director of the school declared our Italian-themed dinner to be one of the best dinners she'd ever eaten. The eggplant timbales that I served up with my fabulous team inspired this recipe. I hope you love it as much as our guests did!

Make-Ahead Tip

You can assemble the timbales and refrigerate them for 2 to 3 days until ready to bake. The Garlic White Bean Dip can also be made in advance and kept refrigerated for 2 to 3 days.

2 large eggplants, very thinly sliced, about ¼-inch-thick lengthwise

Sea salt

2 tablespoons olive oil

1 large onion, finely chopped

8 ounces crimini mushrooms, trimmed and sliced

Sea salt

Freshly ground black pepper

5 ounces baby spinach

1 tomato, finely chopped

2 tablespoons finely chopped fresh Italian parsley or basil, plus extra for garnish

Olive oil

2 cups marinara sauce, purchased or prepared following recipe on page 255

Garlic White Bean Dip (page 27)

Sweat the eggplant: Place eggplant on a baking sheet and salt one side liberally. This will sweat the eggplant and release its bitter juices. After about 20 minutes, wipe the salt and released moisture from the eggplant with a paper towel, or rinse quickly in a colander and pat dry.

While the eggplant is sweating, make the filling by heating 2 tablespoons oil in a large skillet over medium-high heat. Add onions and mushrooms, and sauté until soft. Add 1 tablespoon water at a time if vegetables are sticking to skillet. Season with salt and pep-

(continued on page 167)

Eggplant Timbales (*cont.*)

per. Add in spinach and let wilt, stirring frequently. Stir in tomato and parsley. Remove from heat. Adjust seasoning to taste and set aside.

Preheat a grill or stovetop grill pan. Preheat the oven to 350 degrees. Brush the insides of four medium (6 ounce, 4 inch x 2-inch) ramekins with olive oil.

Brush both sides of the eggplant slices with oil. Grill until each side becomes tender and has prominent grill marks. I use tongs while flipping for best control. Remove from grill.

To assemble the timbales: Place 1 slice eggplant in a prepared ramekin, letting half of it hang over the side. This will be tucked over the filling later. Continue placing more eggplant slices around the bottom of the ramekin (about 4 or 5 slices), overlapping slightly, until the ramekin is completely lined. Fill with mushroom filling. Fold overhanging eggplant flaps over the filling, and tuck ends into the ramekin. Unmold onto a baking sheet. Repeat this process for each timbale and place on a baking sheet. Bake for 5 to 10 minutes, until heated through.

While the timbales are heating, warm marinara sauce in a small saucepan over medium-low heat.

To serve: Ladle 3 tablespoons marinara sauce onto each of 4 individual plates. Spoon 2 tablespoons Garlic White Bean Dip onto the marinara sauce, spreading the dip into a circle slightly larger than a timbale. Lift the timbales from the baking sheet and place one on each mound of dip. Garnish with fresh parsley or basil and serve. Any leftover Garlic White Bean Dip is great on bread!

Green Curry Crepes

MAKES 14 CREPES

If you want a change from curry over rice, you can eat your savory green curry in this garbanzo-flour crepe. Asia meets France in this unique and savory fusion dish.

Make-Ahead Tip

The Green Curry Filling can be made in advance and kept refrigerated for 3 to 4 days.

CREPES

1 cup garbanzo flour	2 cups warm water
1 cup all-purpose flour	2 tablespoons olive oil, plus extra
½ teaspoon curry powder	for pan
1⅛ teaspoons sea salt	1 tablespoon finely chopped fresh
¼ teaspoon freshly ground black pepper	Italian parsley

GREEN CURRY FILLING

2 tablespoons canola oil	1 teaspoon grated fresh ginger
1 large onion, finely chopped	1 teaspoon ground cumin
1 large carrot, peeled and finely diced	1 teaspoon ground coriander
1 russet potato, peeled and finely diced	1 cup vegetable broth, divided
Sea salt	1 15-ounce can chickpeas, rinsed
Freshly ground black pepper	and drained
2 cups packed fresh cilantro leaves and	1 14-ounce can coconut milk
stems	1 tablespoon agave
¼ jalapeño, seeded and minced	1 tablespoon lime juice
3 cloves garlic	5 ounces baby spinach

To make the Crepes: In a blender, combine flours, curry powder, salt, pepper, water, and 2 tablespoons oil. Process just until smooth. Transfer the batter to a bowl and mix in parsley. Let the batter rest for at least 30 minutes.

Heat a lightly oiled 8-inch nonstick skillet or crepe pan over medium-high heat. Pour about ¼ cup batter into pan, while simultaneously tilting the pan around so that the batter coats the whole pan. Let cook for about 1 minute, or until golden on bottom. Gently loosen the edges with a spatula. Flip and cook for another minute until crepe is cooked with small brown spots. Continue making crepes until all batter is used. If batter begins to thicken, add a tablespoon of water at a time to maintain the consistency. To keep crepes hot before serving, see Tip on page 115.

To make the Green Curry Filling: In a large saucepan, heat oil over medium-high heat and sauté onions, carrots, and potatoes until onions are soft and all vegetables are lightly browned, about 10 minutes. Season with salt and pepper.

In the meantime, combine cilantro, jalapeño, garlic, ginger, cumin, coriander, and ½ cup broth in the food processor and process until smooth. Add this spice paste to the saucepan of sautéed vegetables along with the chickpeas, remaining ½ cup broth, coconut milk, agave, and lime juice. Season with ½ teaspoon salt. Bring to a low boil and let cook until mixture is thick and all vegetables are fork tender, about 5 to 10 minutes. Adjust salt and pepper to taste. Add spinach and cook until spinach is wilted.

To serve: Spoon Green Curry Filling over freshly made crepes. Fold one side, then the other, over the filling (fold in thirds), and serve.

Herbed Polenta Cutlets
with Marsala Mushroom Ragout

SERVES 4 to 6

Polenta is a hearty Italian dish made from cornmeal. It is smooth and delicious straight from the pot, but I like to chill it, cut it into shapes, and pan-fry it for a crispy edge. Get in touch with your inner five-year-old and use cookie cutters to try different shapes! Serve the cutlets with a generous topping of sweet Marsala mushrooms and side of Garlicky Greens (page 77) for a beautiful and complete meal.

Note that the cooked polenta will need to chill in the refrigerator for three hours or overnight before continuing with the recipe.

HERBED POLENTA CUTLETS

3½ cups water

1 cup yellow cornmeal, plus extra for dredging

1¼ teaspoons sea salt

½ teaspoon freshly ground black pepper

1 to 2 tablespoons finely chopped fresh herbs, such as Italian parsley or basil

2 tablespoons olive oil

MARSALA MUSHROOM RAGOUT

2 tablespoons olive oil

1 onion, finely chopped

8 ounces crimini mushrooms, trimmed and sliced

8 ounces shiitake mushrooms, stemmed and cut into bite-sized pieces

Sea salt

Freshly ground black pepper

3 cloves garlic, minced

¼ cup Marsala wine

1 cup vegetable broth

2 tablespoons chopped fresh Italian parsley

To make the Herbed Polenta Cutlets: Lightly grease an 8- or 9-inch square pan.

In a medium saucepan, bring water to a boil. Add cornmeal gradually, while whisking vigorously, to avoid clumping. Reduce heat to low, and whisk in salt and pepper. Let cook on low, uncovered, while stirring frequently with a wooden spoon for about 5 to 10 minutes, or until mixture is thick. Turn off heat, stir in herbs, and adjust seasoning to taste.

Transfer polenta to prepared pan and let cool completely. Cover with plastic wrap and chill in refrigerator for 3 hours or overnight until firm.

Remove polenta from refrigerator. Using a 2½-inch cookie or biscuit cutter, cut polenta and remove the discs carefully from the pan with a spatula. Dredge the polenta carefully in cornmeal, tapping off any excess. This will help the polenta to crisp around the edges.

In a large nonstick skillet, heat oil over medium-high heat and pan-fry polenta cutlets in batches. Let cook a few minutes on each side until nicely crisped and golden.

To make the Marsala Mushroom Ragout: In a large skillet, heat oil over medium-high heat; sauté onions and mushrooms until soft. Season with salt and pepper. The skillet may seem overcrowded but, within minutes, the contents of the skillet will shrink down. Add garlic and let cook a few more minutes.

Add wine and broth and bring to a boil. Turn heat to medium-low and let simmer for 20 minutes. Turn off heat and stir in parsley. Adjust seasoning to taste.

To serve: Top each Herbed Polenta Cutlet with Marsala Mushroom Ragout.

Indian Buffet Trio: Saag Aloo, Chana Masala, and Vegetable Biryani, with Garlic Naan

SERVES 6 to 8

Many of my best friends and roomies in college were Indian. They taught me how to dance like a Bollywood star and, more important, how to cook authentic Indian food using everyday ingredients. This trifecta of Indian dishes will blow the minds of vegans and omnivores alike.

Make-Ahead Tip
The Chana Masala, Vegetable Biryani, and Mango Chutney can be made in advance and kept frozen for up to 1 month or refrigerated for 3 to 4 days.

SAAG ALOO

1 large russet potato, peeled and diced

½ cup raw cashews*

½ cup water

1 tablespoon canola oil

1 teaspoon grated fresh ginger

1½ teaspoons curry powder

1½ teaspoons ground cumin

1½ teaspoons ground coriander

5 ounces baby spinach, roughly chopped

3 cloves garlic, minced

Sea salt

Freshly ground black pepper

1 tablespoon tomato paste

CHANA MASALA

2 tablespoons olive oil

1 onion, chopped

Sea salt

3 garlic cloves, minced

1 teaspoon grated fresh ginger

1 teaspoon ground turmeric

½ teaspoon ground cumin

½ teaspoon ground cinnamon

½ teaspoon ground cloves

1 large pinch cayenne

1 15-ounce can chickpeas, rinsed and drained

*If you are not using a high-powered blender, such as a Vitamix, soak cashews overnight or boil cashews for 10 minutes and drain. This will soften the cashews and ensure a silky smooth cream.

2 tomatoes, finely chopped
½ cup water
Freshly ground black pepper
¼ cup finely chopped fresh cilantro

1 tablespoon brown sugar or maple
    syrup
2 teaspoons lemon juice

VEGETABLE BIRYANI
....

2 tablespoons canola oil
1 onion, chopped
3 garlic cloves, minced
1 teaspoon grated fresh ginger
1 teaspoon ground cumin
2 teaspoons curry powder
1 teaspoon ground cinnamon
2 teaspoons sea salt

1½ cups basmati rice, rinsed in a
    mesh sieve and drained
1 tomato, finely chopped
1 cup frozen mixed vegetables,
    such as peas, carrots, green
    beans, and corn
½ cup raisins
1½ cups water
1½ cups vegetable broth

GARLIC NAAN
....

8 garlic cloves, minced
1 to 1½ pounds pizza dough, purchased
    or prepared following recipe on
    page 250

Flour for rolling
2 to 3 tablespoons vegan margarine,
    melted, for brushing

Tamarind-Mango Chutney (page 101),
    optional

To make the Saag Aloo: Place potatoes in a small saucepan and cover with salted water. Bring to a boil and let cook until fork tender. Drain and set aside.

Combine cashews and water in a blender and process on high until very smooth, about 2 minutes. Set aside.

In a large skillet, heat oil over medium-high heat and add ginger, curry powder, cumin, and coriander. Let cook a few minutes until fragrant. Add spinach, garlic, cashew cream, and potatoes, and let cook a few more minutes. Season generously with salt and pepper. Turn off the heat and stir in the tomato paste. Adjust seasoning to taste and serve warm.

(continued on page 175)

To make the Chana Masala: In a large skillet, heat oil and sauté onions over medium-high heat. Season with salt, and let cook until onions are soft and lightly browned. Add garlic, ginger, turmeric, cumin, cinnamon, cloves, and cayenne, and let cook for a few more minutes until fragrant. Add chickpeas, tomatoes, and water. Season generously with salt and pepper. Reduce heat to medium and let simmer for 10 minutes. Mix in cilantro, brown sugar, and lemon juice and adjust seasoning to taste.

To make the Vegetable Biryani: In a large saucepan, heat oil over medium-high heat and sauté onions until soft. Add garlic, ginger, cumin, curry powder, cinnamon and salt; let cook a few more minutes until fragrant. Stir in rice, tomatoes, vegetables, and raisins, and let cook for another minute. Add water and broth and bring to a boil. Reduce heat to low, cover, and let simmer until rice is cooked and liquid is absorbed. Remove from heat and let the rice sit and steam, covered, for 15 more minutes.

To make the Garlic Naan: Preheat the oven to broil.

Knead garlic into the dough until evenly distributed. Divide dough into 6 to 8 equal pieces. Roll each piece into a ball and roll out on a lightly floured surface until about ⅛-inch thick. Place on a broiler pan or baking sheet and brush the top with melted margarine. Broil for 2 minutes, then flip using tongs, and broil for another 1 to 1½ minutes, or until puffed and lightly browned in spots.

To serve: Serve the three dishes together with the Garlic Naan and Tamarind-Mango Chutney for a wonderful buffet.

Mongolian BBQ Seitan

The day that we photographed this dish, the photo team ditched their ordered-in lunches for a plate of my Mongolian BBQ Seitan. This dish is sticky, savory, and sweet, and almost effortless to make.

¼ cup hoisin sauce

¼ cup water

1 tablespoon soy sauce

1 tablespoon agave

1 teaspoon lemon juice

1 to 2 teaspoons chili-garlic sauce

2 tablespoons canola oil

8 ounces shiitake mushrooms, stemmed and sliced

8 ounces seitan, cut into thin strips, purchased or prepared following recipe on page 252

2 teaspoons grated fresh ginger

⅛ teaspoon ground cinnamon

⅛ teaspoon ground cloves

4 ounces snow peas, strings removed

2 scallions, trimmed and thinly sliced

¼ cup chopped fresh cilantro

2 cups cooked rice, for serving

In a small bowl, make the sauce by whisking together hoisin sauce, water, soy sauce, agave, lemon juice, and chili-garlic sauce. Set aside.

In a large skillet, heat oil over medium-high heat and stir-fry mushrooms and seitan until lightly browned and mushrooms have released their juices. Add ginger, cinnamon, and cloves; let cook a few more minutes.

Add the sauce and snow peas to skillet. Reduce heat to medium, and let cook until sauce has thickened. This may happen quickly. Turn off heat and mix in scallions and cilantro. Serve over rice.

Moroccan Bistilla

SERVES 6

A Moroccan bistilla (pronounced bis-TEE-ya) is a cinnamon- and sugar-dusted phyllo pie with a savory filling. The presentation is stunning and the taste is even better. Try belly dancing while you serve it to enhance the Moroccan experience. And don't forget, like all Moroccan food, the proper way to eat this is with your fingers!

Make-Ahead Tip

The filling can be made in advance and kept refrigerated for 2 to 3 days.

2 tablespoons canola oil, plus extra for brushing

1 large onion, finely chopped

8 ounces crimini mushrooms, trimmed and finely chopped

1½ teaspoons sea salt

¼ teaspoons freshly ground black pepper

¼ teaspoon ground turmeric

½ teaspoon ground ginger

½ teaspoon ground cinnamon

1 14-ounce package extra-firm tofu, drained and crumbled

2 tablespoons finely chopped fresh cilantro

1 tablespoon finely chopped fresh Italian parsley

1 cup blanched almonds

½ cup sugar

½ teaspoon ground cinnamon, plus extra for garnish

12 sheets phyllo dough, thawed according to package directions, see Tip (page 37)

Powdered sugar for garnish

In a large skillet, heat 2 tablespoons oil over medium-high heat and sauté onions and mushrooms until soft and lightly browned. Add salt, pepper, turmeric, ginger, and cinnamon. Let cook a few more minutes until fragrant. Stir in tofu and cook for five minutes more. Remove from heat and stir in cilantro and parsley.

Preheat the oven to 375 degrees. Lightly grease a 9-inch round cake pan.

(continued on next page)

Moroccan Bistilla (*cont.*)

In a food processor, pulse almonds, sugar, and cinnamon until the consistency is very fine and crumbly. Set aside.

Lay 2 sheets of phyllo in the bottom of the pan, allowing the edges to come up and over the side of the pan. Brush with oil and sprinkle with 1 tablespoon of the almond mixture. Layer 4 more sheets of phyllo in a circular pattern, so that they overlap in the center and the edges drape over the side of the pan. Brush the top with oil. Add half of the remaining almond mixture to the pan and top with half of the tofu mixture.

Layer 4 more sheets of phyllo in a circular pattern, so that they overlap in the center and the edges drape over the side of the pan. Brush the top with oil. Add the remaining almond mixture to the pan and top with the remaining tofu mixture.

Fold the overhanging edges of phyllo over the top of the tofu filling and brush with oil. Place 2 sheets of phyllo on top, tucking corners in so that the phyllo covers the bistilla, and brush with oil.

Bake for approximately 30 minutes, or until the top is lightly golden. Let cool a few minutes and then run a sharp knife along the inside edge of the pan. Unmold by laying a large serving platter on top of the cake pan and inverting the bistilla onto the platter. The bottom of the bistilla is now the top. Generously sift a thick layer of powdered sugar over the top of the bistilla. If you want to decorate further, lay strips of waxed paper spaced 1 inch apart in a decorative pattern over the top of the powdered sugar and sprinkle cinnamon generously within the spacing. Carefully lift the waxed paper up and you will have a decorative design on the top of the bistilla.

Orange You Glad I Made Crispy Tofu?

SERVES 4

I used to love Chinese fast-food orange chicken before I went vegetarian. I was ecstatic when I found out that this sweet and sticky citrus sauce makes a perfect coating for crispy tofu nuggets. I promise you will be glad you made this almost-too-good-to-be-true dish.

1 14-ounce package extra-firm tofu, drained
1 cup orange juice
Peel from ¼ orange, cut into ¼-inch strips
2 tablespoons agave
1 tablespoon soy sauce
1 teaspoon grated fresh ginger

1 garlic clove, minced
½ teaspoon ground coriander
Canola oil for frying
¼ cup cornstarch or arrowroot
1½ teaspoons sea salt
2 tablespoons chopped fresh cilantro
2 cups cooked rice, for serving

Press the tofu according to directions on page 252. After pressing, cut tofu into ½-inch cubes and set aside.

In a small bowl, mix orange juice, orange peel, agave, soy sauce, ginger, garlic, and coriander. Set aside.

Fill a large heavy-bottomed skillet with ½ inch oil, and heat over medium-high heat. While oil is heating, whisk together cornstarch and salt in a small bowl. Dredge tofu in the flour mixture by tossing a few cubes at a time in the bowl of flour and removing them onto a plate. Be sure to shake off excess flour before frying.

The oil is hot enough when bubbles form around a wooden spoon inserted in the oil. Carefully place tofu in the oil and let fry until the bottom is golden and crisp. Flip tofu using a spatula or tongs and fry until the other side is golden and crisp. Remove tofu from oil and drain on paper towels.

Heat a large skillet over medium-high heat and add fried tofu and orange juice mixture. Let cook until the sauce bubbles down to a thick syrup. Turn off heat and mix in cilantro. Serve over rice.

Pancakes for Dinner

SERVES 2

For those nights when you just feel like eating a big ol' stack of pancakes for dinner. C'mon, admit it. You know you want this tonight! Plus, the batter is super easy to make and oil-free.

1 cup all-purpose flour
1 tablespoon baking powder
½ teaspoon salt
¼ teaspoon ground cinnamon
¾ cup water

3 tablespoons maple syrup, plus extra
   for serving
8 ounces fresh or frozen blueberries,
   optional
Canola oil, for greasing

In a large bowl, whisk together flour, baking powder, salt, and cinnamon. In a separate small bowl, whisk together water and maple syrup. Add the liquid to the flour mixture and whisk until just combined. Do not overmix; the batter should have some lumps.

Lightly oil a large nonstick skillet or griddle and heat over medium-high heat. For each pancake, pour ¼ cup of batter onto the skillet and sprinkle blueberries on top, if using. When small bubbles appear in the center of the pancake, it is time to flip it. Let it cook on the other side until lightly browned and cooked through, about 1 more minute. Repeat with remaining batter, adding more oil to the skillet as needed. If the batter gets too thick, add a little more water, 1 tablespoon at a time. To keep pancakes hot before serving, see Tip on page 115. Serve pancakes with warm maple syrup.

Pineapple Not-So-Fried Rice

SERVES 4 TO 6

Loaded with veggies, tofu, cashews, and raisins, this sweet and salty Thai pineapple rice dish is a healthful and hearty entrée. Who wouldn't love a meal served in a pineapple boat? You'll want to serve this one all the Thai-yum!

1 14-ounce package extra-firm tofu, drained

2 tablespoons soy sauce

1 pineapple, or 1½ cups diced pineapple

1 tablespoon canola oil

1 onion, thinly sliced

Sea salt

3 cloves garlic, minced

2 teaspoons curry powder

1 teaspoon ground coriander

1 teaspoon chili-garlic sauce

¾ cup cashews

1 carrot, peeled and shredded

½ cup frozen peas

½ cup raisins

3 cups cooked rice, preferably jasmine

¼ cup vegetable broth

Preheat the oven to 325 degrees. Grease a small baking sheet.

Press the tofu according to directions on page 252. After pressing, cut the tofu into ½-inch cubes. In a bowl, toss tofu with soy sauce until each cube is coated. Place in one layer on the prepared baking sheet. Bake for 45 minutes, turning the tofu a couple of times with a spatula. Remove from oven and set aside.

To prepare pineapple, cut in half lengthwise using a sharp knife. Remove the flesh and cut into bite-sized pieces. Set aside 1½ cups for this recipe, and save the rest for another use. Reserve the shell for serving.

In a large skillet or wok, heat oil over medium-high heat and sauté onions until soft and lightly browned. Season with salt. Add garlic, curry, coriander, and chili-garlic sauce, and let cook a few more minutes. Add cashews, carrots, peas, raisins, rice, broth, pineapple, and tofu. Cook until heated through and adjust salt to taste. Serve the rice like they do in Thailand—in the pineapple shell!

Seitan Scallopini

SERVES 4

Who says vegan food can't be fancy-schmancy? This ever-so-elegant dish is easy to prepare, but could hold its own in any five-star restaurant. These thinly sliced and battered seitan cutlets basking in a sinfully silky white wine and mushroom sauce can be served with Garlicky Greens (page 77) or Guilt-Free Garlic Mashed Potatoes (page 79).

½ cup all-purpose flour

½ cup water

½ teaspoon sea salt

8 ounces seitan, thinly sliced, purchased or prepared following recipe on page 252

3 tablespoons olive oil, divided, plus extra as needed

1 onion, thinly sliced

4 ounces crimini and/or shiitake mushrooms, stemmed and sliced

Freshly ground black pepper

2 cloves garlic, minced

1 teaspoon dried basil

1 teaspoon dried thyme

1 cup vegetable broth

½ cup white wine

1 tablespoon lemon juice

1 tablespoon finely chopped fresh Italian parsley

Whisk together flour, water, and salt in a small bowl. Dip each slice of seitan in the batter to coat and place on a plate.

Heat 1 tablespoon oil in a large nonstick skillet over medium-high heat and arrange batter-dipped seitan in the skillet in one layer. Do not overcrowd; cook in batches if necessary, adding more oil as needed. Cook seitan for about 5 minutes on each side until both sides are lightly browned and crisp. Set aside to drain on paper towels.

In a large skillet, heat remaining 2 tablespoons oil over medium-high heat and sauté onions and mushrooms until soft and lightly browned. Season with salt and pepper. Add garlic, basil, and thyme, and let cook a few more minutes. Add broth and wine; lower heat to medium. Let cook until liquid reduces to a saucelike consistency. Adjust seasoning to taste. Add pan-fried seitan, lemon juice, and parsley to the skillet. Cook a few more minutes and serve.

Southern Skillet Black-Eyed Peas with Quick Buttery Biscuits

SERVES 4 to 6

This sweet and saucy black-eyed pea dish is so flavorful that it's hard not to eat it straight from the skillet. Serve leftovers in a bun for a Southern-style sloppy Joe. As for the biscuits, they are light, moist, and so easy to make. No rolling or folding technique necessary! Slather them in Whipped Maple Butter (page 29), for the ultimate Southern experience.

SOUTHERN SKILLET BLACK-EYED PEAS

2 tablespoons olive oil

1 large onion, finely chopped

1 green bell pepper, seeded and diced

2 cups cauliflower florets, roughly chopped into ½-inch pieces

2 cloves garlic, minced

1 tablespoon ground cumin

1 teaspoon chili powder

½ teaspoon ground cinnamon

¼ teaspoon cayenne pepper

½ teaspoon sea salt

2 15-ounce cans black-eyed peas, rinsed and drained

1 14-ounce can tomato sauce

1 cup water

¼ cup soy sauce

⅓ cup packed brown sugar or maple syrup

2 tablespoons white or apple cider vinegar

Whipped Maple Butter (page 29)

QUICK BUTTERY BISCUITS

2 cups all-purpose flour, plus extra for work surface

1 tablespoon baking powder

¾ teaspoon salt

½ cup vegan margarine, plus extra for brushing

¾ cup soy, almond, or rice milk

To make the Southern Skillet Black-Eyed Peas: In a large deep-sided skillet or pot, heat oil over medium-high heat and sauté onions and green peppers until soft. Add cauliflower and let cook, stirring frequently, until lightly browned, about 5 to 8 minutes. Add garlic, cumin, chili powder, cinnamon, cayenne, and salt, and let cook a few more minutes.

(continued on page 189)

Stir in black-eyed peas, tomato sauce, water, soy sauce, brown sugar, and vinegar. Reduce heat to medium. Simmer, uncovered, for 15 to 20 minutes, or until cauliflower is fork tender. Adjust seasoning to taste. Serve in soup bowls with Quick Buttery Biscuits and Whipped Maple Butter on the side.

To make the Quick Buttery Biscuits: Preheat the oven to 375 degrees. You can make the dough by hand or using a food processor.

By hand: Whisk together flour, baking powder, and salt in a large bowl. Add margarine and cut it roughly into flour using a pastry cutter, until mixture is the texture of coarse meal with a few larger margarine lumps. Work quickly so that the margarine does not melt. Add nondairy milk and stir with a wooden spoon until just combined. Do not overwork.

Using food processor: Combine flour, baking powder, and salt in the food processor and pulse for about 5 seconds until ingredients are combined. Add margarine and pulse in the food processor until mixture is the texture of coarse meal with a few larger margarine lumps. Work quickly so the margarine does not melt. Add nondairy milk and pulse a few more times until just combined. Do not overwork.

Transfer the dough to a lightly floured surface and pat into an oblong shape, about 1-inch thick. Using a 2½-inch floured cookie or biscuit cutter, cut the biscuits out and place them on a baking sheet. Brush the tops lightly with some melted margarine and bake for about 12 to 15 minutes, or until they begin to turn golden. Remove biscuits from oven immediately and transfer to a wire rack to cool.

Tempeh Piccata

SERVES 4

This scrumptious pan-seared tempeh is dinner-party perfect yet extremely high in protein and fiber. Garnishing with chopped parsley adds an extra oomph to the tangy lemon-caper sauce and makes for a gorgeous presentation. Serve over Garlicky Greens (page 77) or Guilt-Free Garlic Mashed Potatoes (page 79).

1 8-ounce package tempeh, thinly sliced	1 tablespoon cornstarch or arrowroot
4 tablespoons olive oil, divided	2 tablespoons water
1 onion, chopped	3 tablespoons lemon juice
2 cloves garlic, minced	2 tablespoons vegan margarine
Sea salt	2 tablespoons drained capers
Freshly ground black pepper	2 tablespoons chopped fresh Italian
1 cup vegetable broth	parsley

Fill a large pot with enough water to reach the bottom of a steamer basket. Place the tempeh slices in the basket, cover, and steam for 20 minutes. Check the pot occasionally and add more water if necessary. Steaming the tempeh will remove its bitterness.

In a large nonstick skillet, heat 2 tablespoons oil over medium-high heat and arrange tempeh pieces in the skillet. Using tongs or a spatula to flip the pieces, cook tempeh on each side, for 5 minutes, or until nicely browned. Transfer to a plate.

In the same skillet, heat remaining 2 tablespoons oil over medium-high heat and sauté onions until soft. Add garlic and let cook a few more minutes. Season with salt and pepper. Very carefully and slowly add the broth to the skillet, so the oil doesn't spatter. Reduce the heat to medium and let the broth bubble down for 1 to 2 minutes.

Whisk together cornstarch and water in a small bowl and slowly drizzle it into the skillet, mixing continuously until sauce thickens. Add the tempeh to the skillet and reduce the heat to low. Add lemon juice and let simmer for a few minutes, turning the tempeh midway. Turn off the heat and stir in margarine, capers, and parsley until margarine is melted and incorporated. Season again with salt and pepper.

Tropical Island Kebabs with Cilantro Rice

SERVES 4

Fire up your grill and take a tropical getaway with these colorful sweet-and-sour kebabs. It's almost as much fun as swimming with the humuhumunukunukuapua'a, Hawaii's colorful state fish.

Make-Ahead Tip
The Tropical Island Kebabs can be assembled and kept refrigerated for 3 to 4 days until ready to grill. The Sweet-and-Sour Sauce can also be made in advance and kept refrigerated for 3 to 4 days.

CILANTRO RICE
1 cup long-grain white rice

2 cups water

1 teaspoon sea salt

1 tablespoon canola oil

1 tablespoon lemon juice

2 tablespoons finely chopped fresh cilantro

2 scallions, trimmed and thinly sliced

⅓ cup slivered almonds, toasted

TROPICAL ISLAND KEBABS
8 ounces seitan, purchased or prepared following recipe on page 252, cut into 1-inch pieces

½ red onion, cut into 1-inch pieces

1 green pepper, seeded and cut into 1-inch pieces

1 cup pineapple or mango chunks

8 ounces cherry tomatoes

Sweet-and-Sour Sauce (page 256)

To make the Cilantro Rice: In a medium saucepan, combine rice, water, and salt, and bring to a boil. Reduce heat to low and simmer, covered, until rice is cooked and water is absorbed. Remove from heat, and let sit, covered, for 15 minutes. Add oil, lemon juice, cilantro, scallions, and almonds to the rice and fluff with a fork.

To make the Tropical Island Kebabs: Preheat a grill or stovetop grill pan.

(continued on next page)

Tropical Island Kebabs with Cilantro Rice (*cont.*)

Skewer seitan, onion, green pepper, pineapple, and cherry tomatoes in any order. Brush with Sweet-and-Sour Sauce and place on grill. Rotate skewers with tongs until both sides have been cooked and grill marks appear. Remove kebabs from the grill.

To serve: Serve Tropical Island Kebabs over Cilantro Rice and drizzle more Sweet-and-Sour Sauce on top.

Chloe's Kitchen

Cupcakes and More

Baked Sprinkle Doughnuts

MAKES 12 DOUGHNUTS

Why fry doughnuts when they taste even better baked? Plus, baked doughnuts are infinitely easier and more healthful than their fatty deep-fried friends. Nutmeg is the secret ingredient that gives these doughnuts their distinct doughnutty flavor. Top your doughnuts with chocolate or vanilla glaze, and then sprinkle them with your favorite toppings.

2⅔ cups all-purpose flour

⅔ cup sugar

2 teaspoons baking soda

2 teaspoons ground nutmeg

1 teaspoon salt

1 cup soy, almond, or rice milk

¼ cup canola oil

¼ cup white or apple cider vinegar

1 teaspoon pure vanilla extract

CHOCOLATE GLAZE

¼ cup semisweet chocolate chips (dairy-free)

2 tablespoons plus 1 teaspoon soy, almond, or rice milk

½ cup powdered sugar

OLD-FASHIONED GLAZE

1 cup powdered sugar

2 tablespoons soy, almond, or rice milk

Optional toppings: Rainbow or chocolate sprinkles, chopped toasted almonds, shredded coconut, mini chocolate chips.

Preheat the oven to 375 degrees. Lightly grease two doughnut pans.

In a large bowl, whisk flour, sugar, baking soda, nutmeg, and salt. In a medium bowl, whisk nondairy milk, oil, vinegar, and vanilla. Add the wet ingredients to the dry and whisk together quickly until just combined. Do not overmix.

Using a pastry bag or plastic bag with the tip cut, pipe batter into the prepared doughnut pans and bake for 10 to 12 minutes. Remove the pan from the oven and let sit 5 minutes before unmolding.

(continued on next page)

Baked Sprinkle Doughnuts (*cont.*)

To make the Chocolate Glaze: In a double boiler or microwave, melt the chocolate chips and nondairy milk together. Whisk in the powdered sugar until smooth. Let sit for 5 to 10 minutes before glazing so that the glaze thickens and any powdered sugar clumps dissolve.

To make the Old-Fashioned Glaze: In a small bowl, whisk the powdered sugar and nondairy milk until smooth.

To assemble doughnuts: Dip each doughnut into the glaze, covering the top. Twist the doughnut as you remove it from the glaze to give it a nice finish and prevent dripping. Immediately sprinkle the topping onto the glaze and let set.

Chloe's Kitchen

Banana Cupcakes with Lemon Icing

MAKES 18 CUPCAKES

These moist and flavorful cupcakes are iced with light and zesty lemon perfection. Every time I serve these, they disappear without a crumb left behind.

Make-Ahead Tip

The Banana Cupcakes can be made in advance and frozen, unfrosted, for up to 1 month. Thaw and apply Lemon Icing before serving.

BANANA CUPCAKES

2 cups all-purpose flour*

1 cup sugar

1 teaspoon baking powder

½ teaspoon baking soda

1 teaspoon salt

½ teaspoon ground cinnamon

½ teaspoon ground nutmeg

½ teaspoon ground cloves

½ teaspoon ground ginger

1 cup mashed bananas, from approximately 2 very ripe bananas mashed on a plate using the back of a fork

1 cup canned coconut milk, mixed well before measuring

½ cup canola oil

2 teaspoons white or apple cider vinegar

1 tablespoon pure vanilla extract

LEMON ICING

1 cup powdered sugar

3 to 4 teaspoons lemon juice

1 tablespoon water

¼ to 1 teaspoon lemon zest

To make the Banana Cupcakes: Preheat the oven to 350 degrees. Line 2 12-cup cupcake pans with 18 cupcake liners.

In a large bowl, whisk together flour, sugar, baking powder, baking soda, salt, cinnamon, nutmeg, cloves, and ginger. In a separate bowl, whisk together bananas, coconut milk, oil,

*For a gluten-free alternative, substitute gluten-free all-purpose flour plus 1 teaspoon xanthan gum and see page 11.

(continued on next page)

vinegar, and vanilla. Pour the wet mixture into the dry mixture and whisk until just combined. Do not overmix.

Fill the cupcake liners about two-thirds full with batter. Bake for 18 to 20 minutes, or until a toothpick inserted in the center of a cupcake comes out clean with a few crumbs clinging to it. Cool the cupcakes completely before frosting.

To make the Lemon Icing: Whisk the powdered sugar, lemon juice, water, and zest in a small bowl until smooth.

To assemble cupcakes: Spread a thin layer of Lemon Icing over each Banana Cupcake.

Chloe's Award-Winning Ginger Nutmeg Spice Cupcakes

MAKES 18 CUPCAKES

This is my formerly secret winning recipe that took home first prize on the Food Network's Cupcake Wars. It was a case of love at first bite when the judges tasted these Ginger Nutmeg Spice Cupcakes. I have been emailed, begged, and even threatened to reveal this recipe, so here it is!

Make-Ahead Tip

The Spice Cupcakes can be made in advance and frozen, unfrosted, for up to 1 month. The Vanilla Bean Buttercream can be stored in the refrigerator for up to 2 weeks. Thaw cupcakes and frost before serving.

DATE CARAMEL

6 medjool dates

½ cup maple syrup

2 tablespoons water

¼ teaspoon ground cinnamon

SPICE CUPCAKES

2 cups all-purpose flour*

1 cup sugar

1 teaspoon baking powder

½ teaspoon baking soda

1 teaspoon salt

1 teaspoon ground ginger

1 teaspoon ground nutmeg

½ teaspoon ground cloves

½ teaspoon ground cinnamon

1 cup pumpkin puree, canned or cooked fresh

1 cup canned coconut milk, mixed well before measuring

½ cup canola oil

2 teaspoons white or apple-cider vinegar

1 tablespoon pure vanilla extract

*For a gluten-free alternative, substitute gluten-free all-purpose flour plus 1 teaspoon xanthan gum and see page 11.

(continued on page 203)

Chloe's Award-Winning Ginger Nutmeg Spice Cupcakes (*cont.*)

VANILLA BEAN BUTTERCREAM

1 cup nonhydrogenated vegetable shortening

3 cups powdered sugar

1 teaspoon pure vanilla extract

Seeds of 1 vanilla bean

2 to 5 tablespoons soy, almond, or rice milk

To make the Date Caramel: Place dates in a small saucepan with water to cover, and bring to a gentle boil. Let the dates boil gently for 10 minutes. Drain and rinse with cold water until cool to the touch. Peel the dates with your fingers and discard the skin.

Remove the pits and coarsely chop the dates. Place in a blender; add maple syrup, water, and cinnamon. Blend until smooth. Refrigerate until chilled.

To make the Spice Cupcakes: Preheat the oven to 350 degrees. Line 2 12-cup cupcake pans with 18 cupcake liners.

In a large bowl, whisk together flour, sugar, baking powder, baking soda, salt, ginger, nutmeg, cloves, and cinnamon. In a separate bowl, whisk together pumpkin, coconut milk, oil, vinegar, and vanilla. Pour the wet mixture into the dry mixture and whisk until just combined. Do not overmix.

Fill the cupcake liners about two-thirds full with batter. Bake for 18 to 20 minutes, or until a toothpick inserted in the center of a cupcake comes out clean with a few crumbs clinging to it. Cool the cupcakes completely before frosting.

To make the Vanilla Bean Buttercream: Using a handheld or stand mixer, beat the shortening until smooth. With the mixer running on low, add powdered sugar, vanilla extract, vanilla bean seeds, and 1 tablespoon nondairy milk at a time, as needed, until frosting reaches a spreadable consistency. You may not need to use all of the nondairy milk. Beat on high for 2 more minutes until light and fluffy.

To assemble the cupcakes: Spread or pipe a thin layer of the Vanilla Bean Buttercream on the Spice Cupcakes and drizzle with the Date Caramel.

"Chlostess" Crème-Filled Cupcakes

MAKES 14 CUPCAKES

Move over, you other name-brand cupcakes found in a little plastic bag! These are homemade, have half the fat, and are still crème-filled delicious!

Make-Ahead Tip

The Chocolate Cupcakes can be filled with Crème Frosting and frozen for up to 1 month. Thaw cupcakes and apply Chocolate Ganache topping and swirl design before serving. Any leftover Crème Frosting can be stored in the refrigerator for up to 2 weeks.

CHOCOLATE CUPCAKES

1½ cups all-purpose flour*

1 cup sugar

⅓ cup unsweetened cocoa powder

1 teaspoon baking soda

½ teaspoon salt

1 cup cold coffee or water

½ cup canola oil

2 tablespoons white or apple cider vinegar

2 teaspoons pure vanilla extract

CRÈME FROSTING

1 cup nonhydrogenated vegetable shortening

3 cups powdered sugar

1 teaspoon pure vanilla extract

2 to 5 tablespoons soy, almond, or rice milk

CHOCOLATE GANACHE

1 cup semisweet chocolate chips (dairy-free)

¼ cup canned coconut milk, mixed well before measuring

2 tablespoons canola oil

To make the Chocolate Cupcakes: Preheat the oven to 350 degrees. Line two 12-cup cupcake pans with 14 cupcake liners.

*For a gluten-free alternative, substitute gluten-free all-purpose flour plus ¾ teaspoon xanthan gum and see page 11.

(continued on next page)

In a large bowl, whisk together flour, sugar, cocoa, baking soda, and salt. In a separate bowl, whisk together coffee, oil, vinegar, and vanilla. Pour the wet mixture into the dry mixture and whisk until just combined. Do not overmix.

Fill the cupcake liners about two-thirds full with batter. Bake for 16 to 18 minutes, or until a toothpick inserted in the center of a cupcake comes out clean with a few crumbs clinging to it. Cool the cupcakes completely before frosting.

To make the Crème Frosting: Using a handheld or stand mixer, beat the shortening until smooth. With the mixer running on low, add powdered sugar, vanilla, and 1 tablespoon nondairy milk at a time, as needed, until frosting reaches a spreadable consistency. You may not need to use all of the nondairy milk. Beat on high for 2 more minutes until light and fluffy.

To make the Chocolate Ganache: Melt chocolate chips and coconut milk in a double boiler or microwave. Whisk in oil until smooth.

To assemble the cupcakes: Fit a piping bag with a small round or Bismarck tip and fill with the Crème Frosting. Insert the tip into the center of the top of each cupcake and squeeze the bag to fill the cupcake with about 2 to 3 teaspoons frosting. There is no need to scoop out any of the cake. Spread the top of each cupcake with a thin layer of Chocolate Ganache and pipe a 4-loop design with the Crème Frosting.

Chocolate-Chip Brownie Bites

MAKES ABOUT 28 BITES

Kids have a lot of fun making these bite-sized brownie balls and rolling them in powdered sugar. They are perfect for lunchboxes or gifts and can be served in minicupcake papers.

1 cup semisweet chocolate chips (dairy-free)
¾ cup all-purpose flour*
½ cup sugar
2 tablespoons unsweetened cocoa powder
½ teaspoon baking soda
¼ teaspoon salt

½ cup soy, almond, or rice milk
¼ cup canola oil
1 tablespoon white or apple cider vinegar
2 teaspoons pure vanilla extract
1 cup mini semisweet chocolate chips (dairy-free), optional
Powdered sugar for rolling

Preheat the oven to 325 degrees. Lightly grease an 8-inch square pan.

Heat the chocolate chips in the microwave or over a double boiler until melted.

In the meantime, whisk together flour, sugar, cocoa, baking soda, and salt in a large bowl. In a separate bowl, whisk together the nondairy milk, oil, vinegar, and vanilla. Pour the wet mixture into the dry mixture and whisk until just combined. Whisk in the melted chocolate chips and then stir in the mini chocolate chips, if using. Pour batter into the prepared pan and bake for 20 to 30 minutes until a toothpick inserted in the center comes out slightly moist. Remove from oven and let sit until the brownies cool enough to handle.

Scoop about 1½ tablespoons of brownie and roll it into a ball using the palms of your hands. You may want to avoid scooping the crisper edges. Roll the brownie ball in powdered sugar and place on a serving plate or in a mini cupcake paper. Repeat for the remaining brownies.

*For a gluten-free alternative, substitute gluten-free all-purpose flour plus ½ teaspoon xanthan gum and see page 11.

Buckeyes

MAKES 36 BUCKEYES

These chocolate-coated peanut butter candies get their name from the Ohio state tree. They look like the nuts that grow on the buckeye tree, but they taste like peanut-butter cups!

½ cup creamy peanut butter, at room
   temperature
¾ cup powdered sugar

Pinch sea salt
1 cup semisweet chocolate chips
   (dairy-free)

Beat peanut butter in a stand mixer for 1 minute. Add powdered sugar and salt and beat at slow speed until sugar is almost incorporated. Increase speed to medium and beat until ingredients are well combined. Scoop the mixture into 1½ teaspoon balls and place on a parchment-lined plate or tray. Freeze for 15 minutes.

Remove peanut butter balls from the freezer and quickly roll each ball with the palms of your hands to make perfect spheres. Return to parchment-lined tray or plate and stick toothpicks or skewers into each ball. Freeze for 1 hour.

Heat chocolate chips in a double boiler or microwave until melted. Dip each peanut butter ball in the melted chocolate to coat, leaving a small circle of peanut butter uncoated around the toothpick. Return to parchment-lined tray or plate and refrigerate until chocolate sets. Store in refrigerator until serving.

Chocolate Crème Brûlée

This dairy- and egg-free recipe is actually easier to make than traditional Crème Brûlée because you don't have to bother with cracking eggs or baking the custard. The first bite that breaks through the crackly caramelized top, which is made with a torch—how cool is that?—is the best! Pick up a torch at your local kitchen supply or hardware store, and you're ready to make this classic French dessert.

Note that the custard will need to chill in the refrigerator for 8 hours or overnight before torching.

¼ cup soy, almond, or rice milk
¼ cup cornstarch or arrowroot
1 14-ounce can coconut milk
½ cup sugar, plus extra for brûlée

⅛ teaspoon salt
1 cup semisweet chocolate chips
   (dairy-free)

In a small bowl, thoroughly mix nondairy milk and cornstarch with a whisk or fork and set aside.

In a medium saucepan, whisk together coconut milk, ½ cup sugar, and salt, and heat over medium-high heat just until boiling. Reduce the heat to low, and stir in chocolate chips.

Let cook, whisking frequently, until completely smooth. Increase the heat to medium and slowly drizzle the cornstarch mixture into the saucepan, whisking continuously. Let cook until the mixture becomes very thick in texture, about 5 minutes, whisking frequently.

Pour the custard evenly into crème brûlée dishes, ramekins, or coffee mugs. Smooth the tops. Let them cool for 10 minutes; then chill in the refrigerator for 8 hours or overnight.

Remove the custards from the refrigerator 1 hour before torching so that they come to room temperature. Sprinkle about 2 teaspoons sugar onto each ramekin, then give it a little shake so that the sugar spreads evenly.

Hold your torch about 2 to 3 inches from the sugar and melt the sugar until it bubbles and turns slightly golden. Be sure to move your torch back and forth continuously so that it does not burn in one spot. Once there is no more visible dry sugar, let the crème brûlée sit for 3 to 5 minutes and serve immediately.

Note: For an extra-thick, crackly top, add 2 more teaspoons of sugar and repeat the torching process.

Chocolate Molten Lava Cakes with Raspberry Sauce

SERVES 6

Calling all chocoholics! If you like chocolate cake, then you'll adore the journey to the warm melty chocovolcanic center of this luxurious dessert.

Make-Ahead Tip

Ramekins can be filled with the cake batter and frozen for up to 1 month. Bake straight from freezer for 20 minutes.

RASPBERRY SAUCE

1 12-ounce bag frozen raspberries or 2
    cups fresh
2 tablespoons water

½ cup sugar
1 teaspoon lemon juice
⅛ teaspoon salt

MOLTEN LAVA CAKES

1½ cups all-purpose flour
1 cup sugar
⅓ cup unsweetened cocoa powder
1 teaspoon baking soda
½ teaspoon salt
1 cup soy, almond, or rice milk
½ cup canola oil

2 tablespoons white or apple cider
    vinegar
1 tablespoon pure vanilla extract
6 tablespoons semisweet chocolate
    chips (dairy-free)
Powdered sugar for dusting

To make the Raspberry Sauce: In a medium saucepan, cook raspberries, water, and sugar over medium heat for about 15 minutes, or until thick and saucy. Remove from heat and stir in lemon juice and salt. For a smoother sauce, press through a fine-mesh strainer to remove the seeds. Let cool, then store in refrigerator.

To make the Molten Lava Cakes: Preheat the oven to 400 degrees. Lightly grease six 6-ounce ramekins and line the bottom of each ramekin with a small parchment paper circle for easy unmolding.

(continued on next page)

Chocolate Molten Lava Cake with Raspberry Sauce (*cont.*)

In a large bowl, whisk together flour, sugar, cocoa powder, baking soda, and salt. In a separate bowl, whisk together nondairy milk, oil, vinegar, and vanilla. Pour the wet mixture into the dry mixture and whisk until just combined. Do not overmix.

Fill each prepared ramekin one-quarter way full. Place 1 heaping tablespoon of chocolate chips on top of the batter in the center. Fill the ramekins with more batter.

Place the ramekins on a rimmed baking sheet and bake for 15 minutes. Remove from oven and let sit for 3 minutes. Run a sharp knife around the edges of each cake and then gently unmold.

To serve: Sift powdered sugar over the top and drizzle with the Raspberry Sauce. Serve immediately while warm.

Happy Birthday Cake

Birthdays just aren't birthdays without a great cake! Have fun decorating it any way you'd like. My little friends Isabella, Jack, and Vivienne always request this cake on their special day!

This recipe makes two 9-inch round layers. Double the recipe for more layers.

Make-Ahead Tip

The Vanilla Cake layers can be made in advance and frozen, unfrosted, for up to 1 month. The Chocolate Frosting can be stored in the refrigerator for up to 2 weeks. Thaw cakes and frost before serving.

VANILLA CAKE

3 cups all-purpose flour*

2 cups sugar

2 teaspoons baking soda

1 teaspoon salt

1¾ cups soy, almond, or rice milk

1 cup canola oil

¼ cup white or apple cider vinegar

1 tablespoon pure vanilla or almond extract

CHOCOLATE FROSTING

1½ cups semiswet chocolate chips (dairy-free)

1 cup nonhydrogenated vegetable shortening

3 cups powdered sugar

1 teaspoon pure vanilla extract

2 to 5 tablespoons soy, almond, or rice milk

To make the Vanilla Cake: Preheat the oven to 350 degrees. Lightly grease two 9-inch round cake pans or one 9 x 13-inch pan and line the bottoms with parchment paper.

In a large bowl, whisk together flour, sugar, baking soda, and salt. In a separate bowl, whisk together nondairy milk, oil, vinegar, and vanilla. Pour the wet mixture into the dry mixture and whisk until just combined. Do not overmix.

---

*For a gluten-free alternative, substitute gluten-free all-purpose flour plus 1 ½ teaspoons xanthan gum and see page 11.

(continued on page 217)

Fill each prepared cake pan evenly with batter. Bake for 26 to 28 minutes, or until a toothpick inserted in the center of a cake comes out almost clean, with a few crumbs clinging to it. Rotate the cakes halfway through the baking time. Cool the cakes completely before assembly.

To make the Chocolate Frosting: Melt chocolate chips in a microwave or over a double boiler. Let the melted chocolate cool at room temperature for about 10 minutes so that it does not melt the shortening when you add it to the frosting.

In the meantime, using a handheld or stand mixer, beat the shortening until smooth. With the mixer running on low, add powdered sugar, vanilla, and 1 tablespoon nondairy milk at a time, as needed, until frosting reaches a spreadable consistency. You may not need to use all of the nondairy milk. Add the melted chocolate chips. Beat on medium speed until combined. Add more nondairy milk, as needed. Increase speed to high and beat for 2 more minutes until light and fluffy.

> NOTE: For pink vanilla frosting, replace the chocolate chips with a couple of drops of natural red food coloring or 1 to 2 tablespoons thawed frozen raspberries.

To assemble the cake: Once the cakes are completely cooled, run a knife around the inside edge of each cake pan to loosen, and gently unmold the cake. Peel off the parchment paper and slice the dome off the top of each cake. Place one cake on a cardboard cake circle or serving plate, and slide strips of parchment paper under the edges of the bottom of the cake to prevent frosting from getting on the plate. Spread a generous layer of frosting on top of the cake. Place the second cake on top of the first and spread a generous layer of frosting on top. Frost the sides if desired, and remove the parchment paper before serving.

Chocolate Walnut Fudge

MAKES 16 2-INCH SQUARES

Hand to my heart, this fudge is the real deal. Moist, super fudgy, and studded with toasted walnuts, this fudge cannot be beat, even by that nice lady down the street who always made fudge for you when you were a kid. She'll get vegan-envy when you bring some to her!

Note that the fudge will need to chill in the refrigerator for 8 hours or overnight before serving.

- 1 cup canned coconut milk, mixed well before measuring
- 3 cups semisweet chocolate chips (dairy-free)
- 1 tablespoon pure vanilla extract
- 3 cups powdered sugar
- ⅓ cup unsweetened cocoa powder
- 1½ cups walnuts, toasted and roughly chopped

Generously line an 8-inch square pan with foil, so that it covers all sides and hangs over the edges of the pan.

In a small saucepan, heat coconut milk over medium heat until the first sign of boiling. Add chocolate chips and reduce heat to low. Let cook, stirring occasionally, until all chocolate is melted and mixture is smooth. Remove from heat and whisk in vanilla. Set aside.

In the bowl of a stand mixer, combine powdered sugar and cocoa powder. Add the chocolate mixture and beat until all ingredients are incorporated and fudge batter is smooth. Stir in walnuts.

Spread the fudge evenly in the prepared pan. Cover tightly with foil and refrigerate for 8 hours or overnight. Bring to room temperature and cut into 2-inch squares to serve.

Cinnamon-Espresso Chocolate Chip Cookies

MAKES 26 3-INCH COOKIES

These are the best ~~vegan~~ cookies in the world. When I was catering in Los Angeles, I could never fulfill the high demand for these cookies, so I decided to write this cookbook instead. Now you can make them yourself!

Make-Ahead Tip
Cookie dough can be made in advance and kept refrigerated for up to 1 week or frozen for up to 1 month.

2 cups all-purpose flour*
½ teaspoon baking powder
¾ teaspoon ground cinnamon
¼ teaspoon salt
1 cup vegan margarine
3 tablespoons instant espresso powder

1 cup powdered sugar
½ cup packed brown sugar
1½ cups semisweet chocolate chips (dairy-free)
About ¼ cup granulated sugar for sprinkling

Preheat the oven to 350 degrees. Line 2 or 3 large baking sheets with Silpat or parchment paper.

In a medium bowl, whisk together flour, baking powder, cinnamon, and salt.

Using a mixer, beat margarine and espresso powder until well combined. Add powdered sugar and brown sugar, and beat until combined. Mix in the flour mixture ½ cup at a time. If dough seems too dry to scoop, add 1 to 2 tablespoons water. Stir in chocolate chips.

Scoop about 2 tablespoons dough at a time. Roll each scoop in a small plate of sugar. Place each scoop, round side up, on the prepared baking sheets, about 2 inches apart. For crisp cookies, gently flatten the dough with the palm of your hand. For soft cookies, leave as is. Bake about 12 to 14 minutes, or until the edges are browned. Let cool and serve.

*For a gluten-free alternative, substitute gluten-free all-purpose flour plus ½ teaspoon xanthan gum and see page 11.

Hot Fudge Sundaes
with Mint Chip Ice Cream

MAKES 1 QUART

I'll admit it: I'm a bit of a chip snob. I refuse to top my ice cream with chocolate chips from a bag because the chips are just too hard to bite into. I much prefer those thin flecks of chocolate that melt in your mouth, like those you would find in store-bought ice cream. The simple solution is to make them yourself using regular old chocolate chips—it is super easy! I always keep a bag of these homemade chippers in the freezer since I never know when ice cream will be calling to me.

Make-Ahead Tip
Chocolate chips and ice cream can be made in advance and kept frozen. Hot Fudge can be made up to 5 days in advance, refrigerated, and reheated before serving.

MINT CHIP ICE CREAM
1 14-ounce can coconut milk

1½ cups almond milk

¾ cup agave

3 tablespoons canola oil

1 teaspoon pure peppermint extract

⅛ teaspoon salt

¾ teaspoon xanthan or guar gum

1 cup semisweet chocolate chips
   (dairy-free)

HOT FUDGE
½ cup canned coconut milk, mixed well
   before measuring

1 cup semisweet chocolate chips (dairy-
   free)

1 tablespoon agave

½ teaspoon pure vanilla extract

Optional toppings: Coconut Whipped
   Cream (page 239), shredded
   coconut, toasted almonds.

To make the ice cream base, blend coconut milk, almond milk, agave, oil, peppermint extract, salt, and xanthan gum in a blender. Chill in the refrigerator for 2 to 3 hours.

(continued on next page)

While the ice cream base is chilling, make the chocolate chips. Melt chocolate chips over a double boiler or in the microwave. In the meantime, line a baking sheet with Silpat or a piece of parchment paper roughly 16 inches long by 12 inches wide. Using an offset spatula, spread melted chocolate as thinly as possible on the Silpat. Transfer the baking sheet to your freezer shelf for about 15 minutes. When the chocolate is firm to the touch, remove from freezer. With the short edge of the Silpat closest to you, roll it away from your body, like you are rolling a yoga mat or sleeping bag. The chips will break and crackle. The tighter you roll, the smaller the chips. Hold the rolled Silpat over a large bowl and tilt and release the roll to allow the chips to fall into the bowl. Store in freezer.

Once the ice cream base is chilled, prepare it in an ice-cream maker according to manufacturer's instructions. Fold the desired amount of homemade chocolate chips into the ice cream. Cover bowl with plastic wrap, making sure that the wrap is pressed onto the top of the ice cream. Store in freezer.

In a small saucepan, heat coconut milk over medium-high heat until it just boils. Turn heat to low and whisk in chocolate chips. Let cook, whisking frequently, until smooth. Remove from heat and whisk in agave and vanilla.

To assemble the Hot Fudge Sundaes: Assemble your sundae by scooping the Mint Chip Ice Cream into individual bowls. Top with Hot Fudge, Coconut Whipped Cream (page 239), and any other toppings you want, such as shredded coconut or toasted almonds.

Iced Apple Cake Squares

MAKES 1 8-INCH CAKE

When I serve these easy-to-whip-up cake squares to guests, they always ask for seconds and thirds. The cake is extremely moist with a delicate golden crumb and light icing. This is the best version of apple cake I have ever eaten. Nobody will believe that it's vegan, I promise!

2 cups all-purpose flour*
1¼ cups sugar
1 teaspoon baking soda
1 teaspoon ground cinnamon
¼ teaspoon salt
1 cup canola oil
1 tablespoon pure vanilla extract

1 teaspoon white or apple cider vinegar
½ cup chopped walnuts
3 Gala or Braeburn apples, peeled and
    finely chopped
1 cup powdered sugar
2 tablespoons soy, almond, or rice milk

Preheat the oven to 350 degrees. Lightly grease an 8- or 9-inch square pan and line the bottom with parchment paper.

In a large bowl, whisk together flour, sugar, baking soda, cinnamon, and salt. In a separate bowl, whisk oil, vanilla, and vinegar. Pour wet ingredients into the dry and mix until just combined. Do not overmix. Gently fold in walnuts and apples.

Fill prepared cake pan with batter. Bake for about 30 minutes in a 9-inch pan or 45 minutes in an 8-inch pan, or until center is set and the cake is lightly browned on top.

In a medium bowl, whisk together powdered sugar and nondairy milk until smooth. Ice the cake, let set, and cut into squares. Ice the cake while warm or let cool to room temperature.

*For a gluten-free alternative, substitute gluten-free all-purpose flour plus 1 teaspoon xanthan gum and see page 11.

Mocha Almond Fudge Cake

"Whoa! You made that? Yourself?" That's what your friends will be asking when you make this monster of a cake. It is the perfect dessert to show off your rock star, pastry chef skills. Trust me: This one will get you the gig!

Note: This recipe makes two 9-inch round layers. Double the recipe for more layers.

Make-Ahead Tip

The Chocolate Cake layers can be made in advance and frozen, unfrosted, for up to 1 month. The Mocha Frosting can be stored in the refrigerator for up to 2 weeks. Thaw cakes and frost before serving.

CHOCOLATE CAKE

3 cups all-purpose flour*

2 cups sugar

⅔ cup unsweetened cocoa powder

2 teaspoons baking soda

1 teaspoon salt

2 cups cold coffee or water

1 cup canola oil

¼ cup white or apple cider vinegar

1 tablespoon pure vanilla extract

MOCHA FROSTING

1 cup nonhydrogenated vegetable shortening

3 cups powdered sugar

1 teaspoon pure vanilla extract

3 tablespoons instant espresso powder dissolved in ¼ cup water

CHOCOLATE FUDGE SAUCE

1 cup semisweet chocolate chips (dairy-free)

¼ cup canned coconut milk, mixed well before measuring

2 tablespoons canola oil

½ cup almonds, toasted and roughly chopped, for garnish

*For a gluten-free alternative, substitute gluten-free all-purpose flour plus 1½ teaspoons xanthan gum and see page 11.

(continued on next page)

Mocha Almond Fudge Cake (*cont.*)

To make the Chocolate Cake: Preheat the oven to 350 degrees. Lightly grease two 9-inch round cake pans or one 9 x 13-inch pan and line the bottoms with parchment paper.

In a large bowl, whisk together flour, sugar, cocoa powder, baking soda, and salt. In a separate bowl, whisk together coffee, oil, vinegar, and vanilla. Pour the wet mixture into the dry mixture and whisk until just combined. Do not overmix.

Fill each prepared cake pan evenly with batter. Bake for about 30 minutes, or until a toothpick inserted in the center of the cake comes out almost clean, with a few crumbs clinging to it. Rotate the cakes halfway through the baking time. Cool the cakes completely before assembly.

To make the Mocha Frosting: Using a handheld or stand mixer, beat the shortening until smooth. With the mixer running on low, add powdered sugar and vanilla, and beat to incorporate. Add 1 tablespoon of espresso liquid at a time, as needed, until it reaches desired frosting consistency and espresso flavor. Beat on high for 2 more minutes until light and fluffy.

To make the Chocolate Fudge Sauce: Melt chocolate chips and coconut milk in a double boiler or microwave. Whisk in oil until smooth.

To assemble the cake: Once the cakes are completely cooled, run a knife around the inside edge of each cake pan to loosen, and gently unmold the cakes. Peel off the parchment paper and slice the dome off the top of each cake. Place one cake on a cardboard cake circle or serving plate, and spread a generous layer of frosting on top of the cake. Place the second cake on top of the first and spread a generous layer of frosting on top. I like to leave the sides unfrosted. Drizzle the Chocolate Fudge Sauce over the top of the cake vertically and horizontally to make a lattice pattern. Garnish the top of the cake with toasted almond pieces.

Ooey Gooey Cinnamon Rolls

MAKES 12 CINNAMON ROLLS

These should really be called "I can't believe they're vegan Cinnamon Rolls"! They are tender, fluffy, moist, and delicious. No one will ever know that they are not laden with butter and eggs.

Make-Ahead Tip

After the assembled unbaked Cinnamon Rolls have risen, they can be covered in plastic wrap in the pan and refrigerated overnight. Remove plastic wrap and bake the next day according to directions.

CINNAMON ROLL DOUGH

1 cup soy, almond, or rice milk

½ cup plus 1 tablespoon sugar, divided

½ teaspoon salt

8 tablespoons vegan margarine

1 teaspoon pure vanilla extract

¼ cup warm water, about 110 degrees

1 envelope active dry yeast

4½ to 5 cups all-purpose flour, plus extra for rolling

FILLING

¾ cup packed brown sugar

2 tablespoons sugar

1½ teaspoons ground cinnamon

4 tablespoons vegan margarine, melted

1 cup raisins

GLAZE

1½ cups powdered sugar

3 tablespoons water

To make the Cinnamon Roll Dough: In a small saucepan, heat nondairy milk, ½ cup sugar, salt, and margarine over low heat until the margarine is just melted. Remove from the heat and add the vanilla. Let it cool down until warm to the touch about 110 degrees.

While the butter mixture is cooling, place the warm water, remaining 1 tablespoon sugar, and yeast in a 1-cup glass measuring cup. Stir for a second or two and set aside for about 10 minutes. The yeast will get foamy, double in size, and reach the ¾-cup line. If it does not rise in the glass, then the yeast is dead or the water was not at the proper temperature, so try again before proceeding to the next step.

(continued on next page)

Ooey Gooey Cinnamon Rolls (*cont.*)

In a stand mixer with the paddle or whisk attachment, combine the margarine mixture and the yeast mixture, and beat at medium speed for about 1 minute. Reduce the speed to low, and add 2½ cups flour. Mix for about 2 minutes and add 2 more cups flour. Beat for 1 more minute. Remove the dough from the mixing bowl. It will be somewhat wet and sticky. Place it on a floured surface and knead for about 2 minutes with your hands. You can add a little bit of flour to keep the dough from sticking to your hands.

Place the dough in a large well-oiled bowl and rotate the ball of dough so it is completely covered with the oil. This will prevent the dough from sticking to the bowl as it rises. Cover with a dry kitchen towel and place in a warm part of the kitchen. Let it sit until it has doubled in volume, about 1½ hours.

Remove the kitchen towel and punch in the center so that the dough deflates. Take the dough out and put it on a floured surface, cover with the kitchen towel, and let the dough rest for about 10 minutes.

To make the filling and assemble the Cinnamon Rolls: Lightly grease a 9 x 13-inch pan.

Roll the dough out on a lightly floured surface into roughly a 20-inch x 13-inch wide rectangle. No need to measure.

Combine brown sugar, sugar, and cinnamon in a small bowl. Brush or spread the melted margarine over the entire surface of the dough. Sprinkle raisins and the sugar mixture evenly over the surface.

With the long end towards you, roll the dough up evenly. With the seam side down, use a sharp knife to cut the log in half. Then cut each half into six equal pieces. You will have 12 cinnamon rolls. Place the rolls, cut side up, into the prepared pan, in 4 rows with 3 rolls in each row, leaving some space between them. Cover with a towel and place in a warm place until they have risen and expanded, about 1 hour. Meanwhile, preheat the oven to 375 degrees.

Bake, uncovered, for 20 minutes. Let the rolls cool for about 10 minutes.

To make the glaze: Combine powdered sugar and water, and whisk until smooth. Drizzle the glaze over the warm cinnamon rolls. When it sets, the glaze will be smooth and clear.

Sea Salt Toffee Bars

MAKES 16 BARS

These sweet and salty bar cookies make the perfect gift for others, or yourself! Layers of caramel and chocolate atop buttery shortbread are sprinkled with sea salt for some extra-scrumptious pizzazz. If you are like me and love salty food, you will surely love this salty dessert!

SHORTBREAD CRUST

1 cup all-purpose flour

½ cup chilled vegan margarine

⅓ cup powdered sugar

½ teaspoon ground cinnamon

CARAMEL

1 cup packed brown sugar

¼ cup vegan margarine

4 teaspoons soy, almond, or rice milk

1 cup semisweet chocolate chips (dairy-free)

Fleur de sel for sprinkling

To make the Shortbread Crust: Preheat the oven to 350 degrees. Line an 8-inch square pan with foil or parchment paper long enough to overhang the edges.

In a food processor, pulse flour, margarine, powdered sugar, and cinnamon until crumbly. Press into prepared pan and bake for 18 to 20 minutes, or until edges are golden. Remove from oven, let cool, and then chill in refrigerator.

To make Caramel: In a small saucepan, over medium heat, heat brown sugar, margarine, and nondairy milk, stirring frequently. Once mixture comes together, increase heat to medium-high for 1 to 2 minutes, until it begins to boil and the bubbles move into the center of the caramel. Remove from heat and let sit for 10 minutes.

To assemble the bars: Pour the Caramel over the chilled Shortbread Crust. Let cool, and return the pan to the refrigerator to chill.

(continued on next page)

Sea Salt Toffee Bars (*cont.*)

Melt chocolate chips over a double boiler or in the microwave. Evenly spread melted chocolate over the caramel layer. Sprinkle with fleur de sel and return to the refrigerator. Once the chocolate has solidified, lift the cookie from the pan with the foil and remove the foil. With a sharp knife, cut the cookie into 2-inch squares.

Summer Berry Pie à La Mode

MAKES 1 9-INCH PIE

Everyone needs a good old-fashioned pie recipe, and this one hits the spot. The lattice top looks impressive, but it's all an illusion because it's actually a super simple no-weave technique. You can use any fruit you'd like or a combination: apples, blueberries, raspberries, blackberries, peaches, nectarines, cherries—anything goes! For a shortcut, feel free to use store-bought dairy-free piecrust and frozen berries. Let the pie-eating contest begin!

PIECRUST

2½ cups all-purpose flour, or half all-purpose flour and half whole-wheat pastry flour, plus extra for rolling

1 tablespoon sugar

1 teaspoon salt

1 cup nonhydrogenated vegetable shortening or vegan margarine (if using margarine, omit salt)

½ cup ice cold water, as needed

FILLING

¾ cup sugar

¼ cup all-purpose flour

1 teaspoon ground cinnamon

Pinch salt

5 cups fresh or frozen berries (if using frozen, increase flour in filling to ½ cup)

Soy, almond, or rice milk for brushing

Extra sugar for sprinkling

Vanilla Bean Ice Cream (page 238), for serving

Preheat the oven to 375 degrees. Lightly grease a 9-inch pie pan.

To make the Piecrust: You can make the dough by hand or using a food processor.

By hand: In a medium bowl, whisk together flour, sugar, and salt. Using a pastry cutter, cut shortening into flour until mixture has a crumbly consistency. Add ice water, 1 tablespoon

(continued on page 237)

at a time, and mix with a wooden spoon until dough just holds together. You may not need to use all of the water. Do not overwork.

Using a food processor: In a food processor, add flour, sugar, and salt. Pulse until ingredients are combined. Add shortening and pulse until mixture has a crumbly consistency. Add ice water, 1 tablespoon at a time, and pulse until dough just holds together. You may not need to use all of the water. Do not overprocess.

Form the dough into 2 discs and wrap in plastic wrap. Refrigerate for 10 minutes.

Remove 1 disc from the refrigerator. On a lightly floured surface, roll out the dough until it is about ⅛-inch thick. Carefully lift the dough and fit it into the prepared pan, letting about 1 inch hang over the sides. Refrigerate piecrust for 10 minutes.

To make the filling: Whisk together sugar, flour, cinnamon, and salt in a large bowl. Add berries and mix with a large spoon until berries are coated with the dry mixture. Fill the piecrust.

To assemble the pie: Remove the second disc of dough from the refrigerator. Roll it out to ⅛-inch thick and cut out eight 1-inch strips. My lattice technique does not require any weaving. Instead, lay 4 strips horizontally on top of the filling, leaving about ½ to ¾ inch between strips. You may want to use a metal spatula to transfer the dough strips from your work surface to your pie. Lay the remaining 4 strips diagonally over the first 4 strips, creating a diamond shape between strips. Fold the overhanging dough over the edges of the lattice top. Crimp the dough between your two index fingers to make a decorative border.

Brush the top and edges of the piecrust with nondairy milk and sprinkle with sugar for an extra sweet and crisp top. Bake for 50 to 55 minutes, until the crust is nicely browned.

To serve: Top with Vanilla Bean Ice Cream (page 238).

Vanilla Bean Ice Cream

1 14-ounce can coconut milk
1½ cups almond milk
¾ cup agave
3 tablespoons canola oil

Seeds of 1 vanilla bean
⅛ teaspoon salt
¾ teaspoon xanthan or guar gum

Blend coconut milk, almond milk, agave, oil, vanilla seeds, salt, and xanthan gum in a blender. Chill in the refrigerator for 2 to 3 hours. Once the ice cream base is chilled, prepare it in an ice cream maker according to manufacturer's instructions. Store in freezer, wrapped tightly with plastic wrap touching the top of the ice cream.

Tarte Tatin with Coconut Whipped Cream

MAKES 1 9-INCH TARTE

Tarte tatin (pronounced tart ta-TAN) is a fancy French dessert with plump juicy caramelized apples baked on a flaky puff pastry crust. This is apple pie's classy continental cousin, which is sure to impress! Don't be daunted by working with puff pastry; it's much easier than rolling piecrust. Puff pastry can be found in the freezer section near the piecrusts.

Don't forget to make a batch of Coconut Whipped Cream to go with your tarte. This incredible recipe is inspired by my friend Kenda, who made this for me all the time in college.

For best results, Coconut Whipped Cream should chill in the refrigerator for a few hours or overnight before serving.

COCONUT WHIPPED CREAM

1 14-ounce can of coconut milk, chilled, (preferably Thai Kitchen or 365 Whole Foods brand, not lite), NOT stirred

⅔ cup powdered sugar

TARTE TATIN

1 non-hydrogenated puff pastry sheet, thawed according to package directions

4 tablespoons vegan margarine

1 cup sugar

6 Granny Smith or Golden Delicious apples, peeled and quartered

To make the Coconut Whipped Cream: Chill the bowl and whisk of a stand mixer in the freezer for about 30 minutes. If they are not very cold, the cream will not whip properly. Skim the solidified coconut cream off the chilled coconut milk and transfer the solids to the bowl of a stand mixer. Do not include any of the coconut water, even if you have to leave behind a little margin of coconut cream, as even a little bit of coconut water can affect your results. Discard the coconut water or reserve for another use, such as for smoothies.

Add the powdered sugar and whip for a few minutes until the mixture begins to stiffen and turn into whipped cream. Work quickly so everything stays cold. Chill whipped cream in a covered container in the refrigerator. It should firm up even more as it sits in the refrigerator for the next few hours or overnight.

(continued on page 241)

Tarte Tatin with Coconut Whipped Cream (*cont.*)

To make the Tarte Tatin: Preheat the oven to 375 degrees. Remove puff pastry sheet from refrigerator.

In an ovenproof 9- or 10-inch skillet, heat margarine over medium heat until melted. Sprinkle sugar evenly over the melted margarine. Do not mix with a spoon. It is okay if the sugar does not entirely cover the margarine.

Arrange the apples cut side up in concentric circles starting with the outside of the pan and working your way towards the center. You can layer remaining apples on top of the first layer. It will seem like there are too many apples, but they will cook down. Cook on medium-high heat for about 10 to 15 minutes, or until the sugar just begins to caramelize and turn an amber color. Remove from heat.

Lay the sheet of puff pastry over the apples and carefully tuck the ends of the sheet inside the pan edges. With a sharp knife, cut a couple of slits in the center of the puff pastry for venting. Bake for about 30 to 40 minutes, or until the pastry is golden brown and slightly puffed.

Remove the tarte and let sit for about 20 minutes. Run a knife around the edge of the pan to loosen. Place a serving platter on top of the tarte and invert. If a few pieces of apple have remained in the pan, just place them back on top of the tarte. Serve with Coconut Whipped Cream or Vanilla Bean Ice Cream (page 238).

Cupcakes and More

Truffles

Hey, Chef Cupid! Give a box of these homemade chocolates to your special someone on Valentine's Day, and ka-pow—arrow straight to the old ticker! These are inspired by the beautiful handcrafted chocolates that my friend and chocolatier extraordinaire, Sandra, sends me.

½ cup canned coconut milk, mixed well before measuring

Pinch salt

½ teaspoon pure vanilla extract

3½ cups semisweet chocolate chips (dairy-free), divided

Chopped shredded coconut for rolling

Cocoa powder for rolling

In a small saucepan, heat coconut milk over medium-low heat until it just begins to boil. Reduce heat to low and add salt, vanilla, and 1½ cups chocolate chips. Let the chocolate melt, whisking frequently, until smooth. Remove from heat and transfer to an 8- to 10-inch loaf pan. Let cool and refrigerate until firm and set.

Using a small scoop or melon baller, scoop the set chocolate onto a parchment-lined tray and freeze for 15 minutes. Remove from freezer and shape into balls using the palms of your hands. Freeze for 15 more minutes, or until firm.

Melt the remaining 2 cups chocolate chips in a double boiler or microwave. Remove the tray of chocolate balls from the freezer. Dip each ball into the melted chocolate and remove using two forks. If you are making coconut truffles, roll the balls immediately in the shredded coconut until completely coated and then refrigerate. If you are making cocoa truffles, refrigerate the chocolate-coated balls first for about 20 minutes before rolling in the cocoa powder. Refrigerate the truffles until serving.

Yoga Cookies

MAKES ABOUT 32 2-INCH COOKIES

These healthful agave-sweetened cookies are my favorite after-yoga snack. They are loaded with oats, coconut, raisins, walnuts, and chocolate, making them perfect for a boost of energy. I don't know what it is about downward-facing dog that gives me a sweet tooth! Namaste.

Make-Ahead Tip

Cookie dough can be made in advance and kept refrigerated for up to 1 week or frozen for up to 1 month.

- 1½ cups all-purpose flour, or whole-wheat pastry flour
- 1 teaspoon ground cinnamon
- ½ teaspoon salt
- ¾ cup canola oil
- ½ cup agave or maple syrup
- 1 tablespoon pure vanilla extract
- 1½ cups rolled oats
- ½ cup sweetened or unsweetened shredded coconut
- ½ cup raisins
- ½ cup chopped walnuts
- ½ cup semisweet chocolate chips (dairy-free)

Preheat the oven to 350 degrees. Line a large baking sheet with parchment paper or Silpat.

In a large bowl, whisk together flour, cinnamon, and salt. In a separate bowl, whisk oil, agave, and vanilla. Add the wet mixture to the dry mixture and whisk until combined. Using a large spoon or spatula, fold in the oats, coconut, raisins, walnuts, and chocolate chips. Scoop about 1½ tablespoons of cookie dough onto the prepared baking sheet and flatten the dough with the palm of your hand. Bake for 12 to 14 minutes until the edges of the cookies are golden.

Peanut Butter Dog Treats

MAKES ABOUT 50 TREATS

Now, something for our furry friends! There's a whole lot of tail-waggin' and lip-smackin' when my pups smell these all-natural treats baking. These also make great gifts: Wrap these treats and, when you tie them off, attach a dog-bone cookie cutter and a copy of this recipe.

Note: If you do not have a cookie cutter, you can use a small cookie scoop and flatten the dough with the palm of your hand.

2 cups whole-wheat flour
½ cup water, plus extra as needed
⅓ creamy peanut butter, softened

1 tablespoon blackstrap molasses
2 cups vegan carob chips, optional

Preheat the oven to 300 degrees.

In a medium bowl, mix flour, water, peanut butter, and molasses with a spoon until thoroughly combined. Add 1 or 2 more tablespoons water so that dough comes together and is moist. Put the dough on a floured surface and press with your hands until the dough is about ¼ inch thick. Using a 2-inch dog-bone cookie cutter, cut out dog treats, and place them close together on a large baking sheet.

Bake treats for 20 minutes. Turn off oven and leave then in the oven to harden for a few hours or overnight.

When treats are dry and cooled, melt carob chips, if using, in a double boiler or microwave. Dip half of the dog bone into the melted carob and set on a rack to dry. Store in a sealed container at room temperature for up to 2 weeks.

The Basics

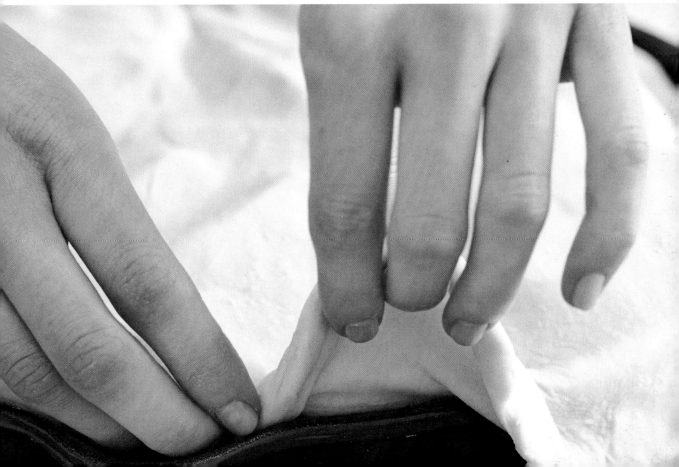

Basic Pizza Dough

MAKES ABOUT 1½ POUNDS

I use this multipurpose pizza dough for homemade pizzas, Garlic Knots (page 25), and even Garlic Naan (page 172). I always keep a batch of this dough in my freezer for sudden carb cravings.

1 ¼-ounce package active dry yeast
1 cup warm water, 110 degrees
2½ cups all-purpose flour, or half all-
  purpose flour and half whole-wheat
  flour, plus extra for rolling

1 tablespoon olive oil, plus extra for
  brushing
1 teaspoon salt
1 tablespoon sugar or maple syrup

In a small bowl, dissolve yeast in warm water. Let stand until bubbles form, about 10 minutes.

In a large bowl, combine flour, oil, salt, sugar, and the yeast mixture. Using lightly floured hands or an electric mixer fitted with a dough hook, mix until a stiff dough has formed. If the dough is too sticky, sprinkle extra flour 1 teaspoon at a time as needed. Place the dough in a large well-oiled bowl and rotate the ball of dough so it is completely covered with the oil. This will prevent the dough from sticking to the bowl as it rises. Cover with a dry kitchen towel and place in a warm part of the kitchen until it has doubled in volume, 1 to 1½ hours. Place dough on a lightly floured work surface, shape into a disc, and knead for five minutes using the steering wheel technique*. Use dough immediately or cover tightly in plastic wrap and refrigerate or freeze for a later use. Thaw to room temperature before using.

*Steering Wheel Technique: Shape dough in a disc and place one hand at 12 o'clock (top of the disc). Fold dough in half toward 6 o'clock. With the heel of your hand, press the dough from 6 to 12 o'clock. Turn dough a quarter of a turn. Repeat process for five minutes.

Chloe's Kitchen

Beans and Grains

Soaking beans helps remove indigestible enzymes that are responsible for gas and bloating. Adding kombu seaweed to the soaking and cooking water also makes beans easier to digest. Lentils and split peas do not need to be soaked.

Beans

If you prefer to cook with dried beans instead of canned, use the following approximation.

½ cup dried beans = 1½ cups cooked beans = 1 15-ounce can beans

Soak the beans in water for 8 hours or overnight with a 3-inch piece of kombu seaweed; discard the soaking water and kombu, and rinse beans.

Place beans and a fresh piece of kombu in a large pot and fill with enough fresh water to cover. Bring to a boil and skim off the foam that rises to the top. Cover, reduce heat to low, and simmer until beans are soft and tender. Cooking time will vary depending on the amount and type of bean. Do not boil vigorously because the beans will burst and become mushy. If water begins to evaporate, add more hot water. Add ¼ teaspoon sea salt per cup of dried beans in the last 10 minutes of cooking.

Grains

Rinse and drain grains before cooking. The general ratio for cooking grains is 1 part grain to 2 parts water. One cup of uncooked grains makes approximately 3 cups cooked grains.

Bring water to a boil in a medium saucepan and add 1 teaspoon sea salt. Add grains, cover with a tightly fitting lid, and reduce heat to low. Simmer until grains are tender and water has absorbed. Remove from heat and let steam, covered, for 10 to 15 minutes. Cooking time will vary depending on the amount and type of grain. Do not stir grains or they will become mushy; instead, fluff with a fork.

Homemade Seitan

MAKES ABOUT 1½ POUNDS

While there is nothing wrong with buying packaged seitan, making your own is more cost efficient and fun!

1⅓ cups vital wheat gluten
1 cup water

4 cups vegetable broth
¼ cup soy sauce

In a large bowl, combine vital wheat gluten and water. Knead for 5 minutes, or until a stiff dough has formed. The dough will be very tough. Let rest for 5 minutes.

In the meantime, combine broth and soy sauce in a large saucepan. Cut the seitan dough in half and place the two pieces in the saucepan. Bring to a boil, then reduce heat to low and simmer, covered, for 30 minutes. Turn over the pieces of dough and simmer for 30 minutes more. Remove from heat, uncover, and let cool in broth. Seitan is now ready to be cubed or sliced for any recipe. Store leftover seitan in broth in the refrigerator for up to 3 days or remove from broth, wrap tightly, and freeze for up to 3 weeks.

Pressing Tofu

Forget any notions of tofu tasting bland or rubbery! Here is the trick to flavorful tofu.

Tofu retains a lot of water, so pressing out the water allows the tofu to take on more flavor from your dish. Take a block of extra-firm tofu and wrap it tightly in dry paper towels or a clean kitchen towel. Set the tofu on a flat surface and place a small baking pan on top. Then stack something heavy, like canned food or books, on top. Let the tofu sit for 20 minutes while it releases its water. Now your tofu is ready to soak up all the delicious juices and flavors from your dish!

Sweet Tomato Ketchup

MAKES ABOUT 1 CUP

There's nothing wrong with using bottled ketchup, but this recipe is so easy and has a delicious and distinct tomato flavor. It is sweetened naturally with agave and the addition of cayenne pepper kicks up the heat. It will keep for up to a week in your refrigerator. The ketchup is best served chilled, so make it the day before or far enough ahead that it can be chilled for at least four hours.

1 cup tomato puree
¼ cup agave
1 clove garlic, pressed
2 tablespoons plus 2 teaspoons white or
  apple cider vinegar

1 teaspoon sea salt
¼ teaspoon ground cinnamon
½ teaspoon onion powder
⅛ teaspoon cayenne pepper, optional

In a medium saucepot, combine tomato puree, agave, garlic, 2 tablespoons vinegar, salt, cinnamon, onion powder, and cayenne, and bring to a boil. Simmer on low for 30 minutes, or until the mixture thickens. Whisk in remaining 2 teaspoons vinegar. Let cool and chill in the refrigerator. Serve in small dishes or dispense from a plastic squeeze bottle.

Sour Cream

MAKES ABOUT ¾ CUP

I absolutely love this homemade Sour Cream. Use it as a fresh topping on tacos, burritos, or baked potatoes!

6 ounces soft tofu
¼ cup olive oil
1 clove garlic

2 teaspoons Dijon mustard
1 tablespoon lemon juice
½ teaspoon sea salt

Puree tofu, oil, garlic, mustard, lemon juice, and salt in a blender until smooth. Store in refrigerator.

Barbecue Sauce

MAKES ABOUT 3 CUPS

This recipe is so delicious that you might just need a straw.

2 cups ketchup, purchased, or prepare
    double the recipe on page 253
½ cup water
½ cup apple cider vinegar
½ cup packed brown sugar or maple
    syrup

2 teaspoons Dijon mustard
2 teaspoons onion powder
1 teaspoon freshly ground black
    pepper
1 tablespoon lemon juice

Combine all ingredients in a medium saucepan and bring to a boil. Reduce heat to low and simmer, uncovered, for 30 minutes.

Marinara Sauce

Everybody needs a homemade marinara sauce recipe that's quick and easy. This one has a little bit of sweetness that makes it irresistible.

2 tablespoons olive oil
1 onion, finely chopped
1 large carrot, peeled and finely chopped
1 cup finely chopped celery
2 garlic cloves, minced
2 teaspoons Italian seasoning

½ teaspoon sea salt
½ teaspoon freshly ground black pepper
1 28-ounce can crushed tomatoes
¼ cup soy, almond, or rice milk
1 tablespoon brown sugar or maple syrup

Heat oil in a large saucepan over medium heat. Add onions, carrots, and celery and sauté until onions are soft and vegetables are lightly browned. Add garlic, Italian seasoning, salt, and pepper, and let cook a few more minutes. Add crushed tomatoes and bring to a boil. Reduce heat to low and simmer, uncovered, for 15 minutes, or until the sauce thickens.

Remove from heat and stir in nondairy milk and brown sugar, which will soften the acidity of the tomatoes. Adjust seasoning to taste.

Sweet-and-Sour Sauce

MAKES ABOUT 1½ CUPS

Pour this sauce over just about anything for a sweet and satisfying meal: veggies, rice, tofu, anything goes! You can also use it in my recipes for Tropical Island Kebabs with Cilantro Rice (page 193) and Sweet-and-Sour Party Meatballs (page 33).

¾ cup water
½ cup packed brown sugar or maple syrup
¼ cup white or apple cider vinegar
¼ cup soy sauce

3 tablespoons ketchup, purchased or prepared following recipe on page 253
2 tablespoons cornstarch or arrowroot

In a medium saucepan, whisk together water, brown sugar, vinegar, soy sauce, ketchup, and cornstarch. Heat the sauce over medium-high heat until it comes to a boil. Reduce the heat to medium-low and cook, whisking frequently, until the mixture has thickened and big syrupy bubbles appear on the surface.

Soy-Free Soy Sauce

MAKES 1 CUP

I could not find bottled soy-free soy sauce, so I decided to craft my own for those who are allergic to soy.

1 cup vegetable broth
1 tablespoon balsamic vinegar
2 teaspoons molasses

2 teaspoons sea salt
Pinch ground ginger
Pinch garlic powder

In a small saucepan, combine all ingredients and whisk together until combined. Bring to a boil over medium-high heat, whisking frequently. Reduce heat to medium, and let boil gently for 5 minutes. Remove from heat and let cool. Store in the refrigerator in an airtight container for up to a week.

Toasting Nuts

Spread the nuts in one layer on a rimmed baking sheet and bake at 350 degrees for about 8 to 12 minutes, or until lightly browned and fragrant. Transfer nuts to a bowl; they will continue to cook a bit after you remove them from the heat.

Menu Suggestions

Weeknight Italian

Garlic White Bean Dip, *page 27*

Orecchiette in No-Cook Spinach Sauce, *page 131*

Cinnamon-Espresso Chocolate Chip Cookies, *page 221*

Date Night

Simple Side Salad with Shallot-Dijon Vinaigrette, *page 62*

Penne alla Vodka with the Best Garlic Bread in the World, *page 143*

Chocolate Crème Brûlée, *page 210*

Potluck Dishes

Kalamata Olive Tapenade, *page 27*

Artichoke-Walnut Pesto Crostini, *page 15*

Phyllo Mushroom Turnovers, *page 36*

Easy Peasy Pasta Salad, *page 57*

Peanutty Perfection Noodles, *page 141*

Ooh-La-La Lasagna, *page 136*

Chocolate Walnut Fudge, *page 219*

Cinnamon-Espresso Chocolate Chip Cookies, *page 221*

Kids Birthday Party

Sweet-and-Sour Party Meatballs, *page 33*

Best-Ever Baked Macaroni and Cheese, *page 127*,
or Easy Peasy Pasta Salad, *page 57*

Happy Birthday Cake, *page 215*

"Chlostess" Crème-Filled Cupcakes, *page 205*

Holiday Feast

Country Meatloaf and Golden Gravy with Orange-Scented
Cranberry Sauce, *page 161*

Guilt-Free Garlic Mashed Potatoes, *page 79*,
or Thyme for Creamy Scalloped Potatoes, *page 89*

Coconut Mashed Yams with Currants, *page 73*

Maple-Roasted Brussels Sprouts with Toasted Hazelnuts, *page 81*

Chloe's Award-Winning Ginger Nutmeg Spice Cupcakes, *page 201*

Iced Apple Cake Squares, page 225

Game Day

Warm Spinach-Artichoke Dip, *page 41*

Mini Potato Skins Stuffed with Avocado Salsa, *page 31*

Sea Salt and Vinegar French Fries, *page 87*

Falafel Sliders with Avocado Hummus, *page 107*

Buckeyes, *page 209*

Chocolate Chip Brownie Bites, *page 207*

Comfy Cozy Southern Supper

Jalapeño Cornbread Poppers with Whipped Maple Butter, *page 29*

Garlicky Greens, *page 77*

Best-Ever Baked Macaroni and Cheese, *page 127*,
or Southern Skillet Black-Eyed Peas with Quick Buttery Biscuits, *page 187*

Summer Berry Pie à La Mode, *page 235*

Teen Slumber Party

Garlic Knots, *page 25*

Caesar Salad with Maple-Wheat Croutons, *page 47*

Spaghetti Bolognese, *page 145*

Hot Fudge Sundaes with Mint Chip Ice Cream, *page 223*

Pancakes for Dinner, *page 183* (for the next morning)

Ladies Lunch

Minted Couscous with Arugula, Butternut Squash, and Currants, *page 61*

Grilled Lemon–Olive Oil Asparagus, *page 78*

Tomato-Basil Bisque with Pumpernickel Croutons, *page 63*

Banana Cupcakes with Lemon Icing, *page 199*

Truffles, *page 243*

Light Lunchbox

Mandarin Peanut-Crunch Salad with Crispy Wontons, *page 59*
(dressing on the side)

Wasabi Sesame Noodle Salad, *page 68*,
or Peanutty Perfection Noodles, *page 141*

Yoga Cookies, *page 245*

Acknowledgments

A big thank you to:

My trailblazing editors, Leslie Meredith and Dominick Anfuso, and the entire Free Press, Simon & Schuster family for making this book possible. You kept me well fed with vegan pastries at every meeting.

Eric Lupfer, my wonderful agent at William Morris Endeavor for patiently walking me through this new experience.

The two most important men in my life: my loving dad, Don, who supports and guides me every day, and my big brother Andy, who always keeps me laughing and has tasted every single recipe in this book . . . over and over and over again.

Photographer Miki Duisterhof, prop stylist Nan Whitney, and food stylist Paul Lowe. It was so sweet that you guys insisted on eating vegan every day during our two-week shoot in New York.

Photographer Richard Reinsdorf, for having great energy and creative ideas.

Paula Jacobson and Sheilah Kaufman, my tireless recipe testers, for testing the sweet potato gnocchi until it was coming out of their ears!

Sandhya Jacob, loyal to the end, I never could have done this without you.

Sonia and Mahshid Sohaili, my fellow mother-daughter dynamo team, I love you both.

Ultrahip fashion stylist, Ava E. Naimi. You taught me that my colors are bright orange and pink. Who knew?

Neil D. Barnard, M.D., for sharing your groundbreaking medical knowledge with my readers.

Thanks and hugs to: *VegNews* magazine, Carisa Hays, Lisa Bloom, The Natural Gourmet Institute, the Hartman family, the Welsh family, the Iezman Family, Aaron Lea, CJ Yu, Linda Wolvek, Robert Raphael, Cean Okada, Anna Bolek, Teri Lyn Fisher, Jenny Park, Deepti Chauhan, and my grandfather, Dac Coscarelli.

Pastry Chef Anne Baptiste at Millennium Restaurant. I called you one morning and asked if I could be your intern, and the rest is history. Thank you for being a role model.

Nothing is possible without great friends, and I am so lucky to have the best in the world. LA girls, Berkeley girls, and my cooking school friends from CTP177, I love you all!

Last, but not least, I would like to thank you! Thank you for picking up this book and believing in my recipes. It is because of you that we can all work together to spread health and happiness through the food we cook.

Index

Note: Page references in *italics* indicate photographs.

A

agave, about, 9
almond milk, about, 7
almond(s)
  fudge cake, mocha, *226,*
    227–28
  Moroccan bistilla, *178,*
    179–80
apple(s)
  cake squares, iced, 225
  lentil, and squash stew,
    curried, *54,* 55
  tarte tatin with coconut
    whipped cream, 239–41,
    240
apricot-mustard sauce, wontons
  with, *42,* 43–44
arrowroot, about, 9
artichoke(s)
  fire-roasted, with garlic oil,
    74, 75–76
  -spinach dip, warm, *40,* 41
  -walnut pesto crostini, *14,* 15
asparagus
  grilled lemon–olive oil, 78
  pasta Italiano, 138
  trimming ends of, 78
avocado(s)
  Chloe's favorite five-minute
    salad, 53
  cutting, 32
  hummus, falafel sliders with,
    106, 107–8
  pesto pasta, *124,* 125
  salsa, mini potato skins
    stuffed with, *30,* 31–32
  -shiitake sushi, 16–17, *17*
  toast, *94,* 95

B

balsamic bruschetta, 19
banana cupcakes with lemon
  icing, 199–200
barbecue sauce, 254

barley bliss casserole, 158
basil
  avocado pesto pasta, *124,*
    125
  balsamic bruschetta, 19
  grilled pesto pizza with
    sweet potatoes, kale, and
    balsamic reduction, 98–99
  ooh-la-la lasagna, 136–37
  stuffed shells with arrabbiata
    sauce, *148,* 149–50
  -tomato bisque with
    pumpernickel croutons,
    63–65, *64*
BBQ pineapple pizza, *96,* 97
BBQ seitan, Mongolian, *176,*
  177
bean(s)
  barley bliss casserole, 158
  black, baby cakes with
    pineapple salsa, 20–21
  California chipotle chop
    with agave-lime
    vinaigrette, 49
  Caribbean vegetables
    with coconut rice and
    plantains, 159–60
  Chloe's award-winning
    mango masala panini, *100,*
    101–2
  falafel sliders with avocado
    hummus, *106,* 107–8
  green curry crepes, 168–69
  and greens soup, Tuscan,
    over garlic toast, 66–67
  Indian buffet trio: saag
    aloo, chana masala, and
    vegetable biryani, with
    garlic naan, 172–75, *174*
  LA-style chimichurri tacos,
    109–11, *110*
  orecchiette in no-cook
    spinach sauce, 131
  pasta Italiano, 138

  soaking and cooking, 251
  southern skillet black-eyed
    peas with quick buttery
    biscuits, 187–89, *188*
  spaghetti bolognese, 145
  Thai chickpea burgers with
    sweet 'n' spicy sauce,
    121–22
  white, dip, garlic, 27
berry pie, summer, à la mode,
  235–37, *236*
biscuits, quick buttery,
  187–89, *188*
black-eyed peas, southern
  skillet, with quick buttery
  biscuits, 187–89, *188*
bread(s)
  artichoke-walnut pesto
    crostini, *14,* 15
  balsamic bruschetta, 19
  crumbs, gluten-free, about,
    12
  garlic, the best in the world,
    142, 144
  garlic knots, *24,* 25–26
  garlic naan, 173–75, *174*
  gluten-free, about, 11
  ooey gooey cinnamon rolls,
    229–31, *230*
  quick buttery biscuits, 187–
    189, *188*
  sourdough, bowls, cheesy
    broccoli soup in, *50,* 51
  Tuscan bean and greens soup
    over garlic toast, 66–67
broccoli
  Caribbean vegetables
    with coconut rice and
    plantains, 159–60
  Chinese takeout chow mein,
    128, 129–30
  classic roasted vegetables, 71
  soup, cheesy, in sourdough
    bread bowls, *50,* 51

brownie bites, chocolate-chip, 207
brown rice noodles, about, 8
bruschetta, balsamic, 19
brussels sprouts, maple-roasted, with toasted hazelnuts, 80, 81–82
buckeyes, 208, 209
burgers
  double double drive-thru, 103–5, 104
  falafel sliders with avocado hummus, 106, 107–8
  Thai chickpea, with sweet 'n' spicy sauce, 121–22

C
cabbage
  Mandarin peanut-crunch salad with crispy wontons, 58, 59
  moo shu vegetables with homemade Chinese pancakes, 112, 113–14
Caesar salad with maple-wheat croutons, 46, 47–48
cakes
  chocolate molten lava, with raspberry sauce, 212, 213–14
  happy birthday, 215–17, 216
  iced apple cake squares, 225
  mocha almond fudge, 226, 227–28
canola oil, about, 1
capers, about, 3
Caribbean vegetables with coconut rice and plantains, 159–60
cashew(s)
  fettuccine alfredo, 134, 135
  pineapple not-so-fried rice, 184, 185
  -shiitake, broth, drunken noodles in, 132, 133
  thyme for creamy scalloped potatoes, 88, 89
  wontons with apricot-mustard sauce, 42, 43–44

cauliflower
  Chloe's award-winning mango masala panini, 100, 101–2
  classic roasted vegetables, 71
  guilt-free garlic mashed potatoes, 79
  samosas with cilantro-tamarind dipping sauce, 38–39
  southern skillet black-eyed peas with quick buttery biscuits, 187–89, 188
cheesy broccoli soup in sourdough bread bowls, 50, 51
chiffonade, about, 77
chili-garlic sauce, about, 3
Chinese takeout boxes, 130
Chinese takeout chow mein, 128, 129–30
Chloe's award-winning ginger nutmeg spice cupcakes, 201–3, 202
Chloe's award-winning mango masala panini, 100, 101–2
Chloe's favorite five-minute salad, 53
"Chlostess" crème-filled cupcakes, 204, 205–6
chocolate
  baked sprinkle doughnuts, 196, 197–98
  buckeyes, 208, 209
  -chip brownie bites, 207
  chip cookies, cinnamon-espresso, 220, 221
  chips, about, 3
  "Chlostess" crème-filled cupcakes, 204, 205–6
  crème brûlée, 210–11
  happy birthday cake, 215–17, 216
  mocha almond fudge cake, 226, 227–28
  molten lava cakes with raspberry sauce, 212, 213–14
  sea salt toffee bars, 232, 233–34

truffles, 242, 243
walnut fudge, 218, 219
yoga cookies, 245
cilantro
  green curry crepes, 168–69
  LA-style chimichurri tacos, 109–11, 110
  rice, tropical island kebabs with, 192, 193–94
  -tamarind dipping sauce, samosas with, 38–39
cinnamon
  -espresso chocolate chip cookies, 220, 221
  rolls, ooey gooey, 229–31, 230
coconut
  milk, about, 7
  oil, about, 1
  rice and plantains, Caribbean vegetables with, 159–60
  truffles, 242, 243
  whipped cream, tarte tatin with, 239–41, 240
  yoga cookies, 245
cookies
  cinnamon-espresso chocolate chip, 220, 221
  yoga, 245
cornbread poppers, jalapeño, with whipped maple butter, 28, 29
cornmeal
  about, 5
  herbed polenta cutlets with marsala mushroom ragout, 170–71
  jalapeño cornbread poppers with whipped maple butter, 28, 29
cornstarch, about, 9
couscous, minted, with arugula, butternut squash, and currants, 60, 61
cranberry sauce, orange-scented, country meatloaf and golden gravy with, 161–64, 162
crème brûlée, chocolate, 210–11

crepes
    green curry, 168–69
    keeping hot, 115
crostini, artichoke-walnut pesto, *14, 15*
cucumbers
    shredding, 68
    wasabi sesame noodle salad, 68
cupcakes
    banana, with lemon icing, 199–200
    "Chlostess" crème-filled, *204,* 205–6
    ginger nutmeg spice, Chloe's award-winning, 201–3, *202*
currants
    arugula, and butternut squash, minted couscous with, *60,* 61
    coconut mashed yams with, *72, 73*
curried dishes
    Chloe's award-winning mango masala panini, *100,* 101–2
    curried lentil, squash, and apple stew, *54, 55*
    green curry crepes, 168–69
    Indian buffet trio: saag aloo, chana masala, and vegetable biryani, with garlic naan, 172–75, *174*
    pineapple not-so-fried rice, *184, 185*
    samosas with cilantro-tamarind dipping sauce, 38–39

D
dips and spreads
    garlic white bean dip, 27
    kalamata olive tapenade, 27
    warm spinach-artichoke dip, *40,* 41
doughnuts, baked sprinkle, *196,* 197–98
drunken noodles in cashew-shiitake broth, *132,* 133

E
eggplant
    miso-glazed, *84, 85*
    timbales, 165–67, *166*
equipment, 10
espresso
    about, 3
    -cinnamon chocolate chip cookies, *220, 221*
    mocha almond fudge cake, *226,* 227–28

F
falafel sliders with avocado hummus, *106,* 107–8
flour, about, 5
flour, gluten-free, about, 11
food processor, 10
fudge, chocolate walnut, *218,* 219

G
garbanzo flour, about, 5
garlic
    bread, the best in the world, *142,* 144
    garlicky greens, 77
    knots, *24, 25–26*
    mashed potatoes, guilt-free, 79
    naan, 173–75, *174*
    oil, fire-roasted artichokes with, *74, 75–76*
    rosemary tomato galette with pine nut ricotta, 117–20, *118*
    toast, Tuscan bean and greens soup over, 66–67
    white bean dip, 27
ginger nutmeg spice cupcakes, Chloe's award-winning, 201–3, *202*
gluten-free substitutes, 11–12
gnocchi, sweet potato, with sage butter, 151–52, *153*
grains
    cooking, 251
    types of, 5
    see also specific grains

greens
    and bean soup, Tuscan, over garlic toast, 66–67
    Caesar salad with maple-wheat croutons, *46,* 47–48
    California chipotle chop with agave-lime vinaigrette, 49
    Chloe's favorite five-minute salad, *53*
    garlicky, 77
    grilled pesto pizza with sweet potatoes, kale, and balsamic reduction, 98–99
    Mandarin peanut-crunch salad with crispy wontons, *58, 59*
    simple side salad with shallot-dijon vinaigrette, 62

H
hazelnuts
    toasted, maple-roasted brussels sprouts with, *80,* 81–82
    toasting, 82
herb(ed)
    cutting in chiffonade, 77
    polenta cutlets with marsala mushroom ragout, 170–71
    see also specific herbs
hoisin sauce, about, 3, 12

I
ice cream
    mint chip, hot fudge sundaes with, *222,* 223–24
    vanilla bean, 238
ice cream maker, 10
Indian buffet trio: saag aloo, chana masala, and vegetable biryani, with garlic naan, 172–75, *174*

J
jalapeño cornbread poppers with whipped maple butter, *28, 29*

K

kale
    garlicky greens, 77
    sweet potatoes, and balsamic
        reduction, grilled pesto
        pizza with, 98–99
ketchup, sweet tomato, 253

L

lasagna, ooh-la-la, 136–37
leek(s)
    cleaning, 23
    -potato patties, crispy, with
        lemon-dill dip, 22–23
legumes, 5
    see also bean(s); lentil(s)
lemon
    -dill dip, crispy potato-leek
        patties with, 22–23
    icing, banana cupcakes with,
        199–200
    –olive oil asparagus, grilled,
        78
lentil(s)
    double double drive-thru
        burgers, 103–5, 104
    squash, and apple stew,
        curried, 54, 55
    sweet-and-sour party
        meatballs, 33–35, 34

M

mango(es)
    cutting, 102
    masala panini, Chloe's
        award-winning, 100,
        101–2
maple (syrup)
    about, 9
    butter, whipped, jalapeño
        cornbread poppers with,
        28, 29
    Chloe's award-winning
        ginger nutmeg spice
        cupcakes, 201–3, 202
    -roasted brussels sprouts
        with toasted hazelnuts,
        80, 81–82
    -wheat croutons, Caesar
        salad with, 46, 47–48
margarine, vegan, buying, 1, 12

marinara sauce, 255
meatballs, sweet-and-sour party,
    33–35, 34
meatloaf, country, and golden
    gravy with orange-
    scented cranberry sauce,
    161–64, 162
meat substitutes, about, 6–7
milk, nondairy, varieties of, 7
minted couscous with arugula,
    butternut squash, and
    currants, 60, 61
mirin, about, 3
miso, about, 4
    miso-glazed eggplant, 84,
        85
mixers, stand or hand, 10
mocha almond fudge cake, 226,
    227–28
Mongolian BBQ seitan, 176,
    177
moo shu vegetables with
    homemade Chinese
    pancakes, 112, 113–14
Moroccan bistilla, 178, 179–80
mushroom(s)
    about, 6 7
    avocado-shiitake sushi,
        16–17, 17
    barley bliss casserole, 158
    Chinese takeout chow
        mein, 128, 129–30
    drunken noodles in cashew-
        shiitake broth, 132, 133
    eggplant timbales, 165–67,
        166
    LA-style chimichurri tacos,
        109–11, 110
    marsala ragout, herbed
        polenta cutlets with,
        170–71
    Mongolian BBQ seitan, 176,
        177
    moo shu vegetables with
        homemade Chinese
        pancakes, 112, 113–14
    Moroccan bistilla, 178,
        179–80
    ooh-la-la lasagna, 136–37
    portobello pesto panini,
        116

seitan scallopini, 186
spaghetti bolognese, 145
straw and hay pasta, 146,
    147
teriyaki wok vegetables, 83
turnovers, phyllo, 36–37
wild, stroganoff fettuccine,
    154, 155
wontons with apricot-
    mustard sauce, 42, 43–44

N

noodle(s)
    Chinese takeout chow mein,
        128, 129–30
    drunken, in cashew-shiitake
        broth, 132, 133
    peanutty perfection, 140,
        141
    salad, wasabi sesame, 68
    types of, 8
nutritional yeast flakes
    about, 4
    barley bliss casserole, 158
    best-ever macaroni and
        cheese, 126, 127
    the best garlic bread in the
        world, 142, 144
    cheesy broccoli soup in
        sourdough bread bowls,
        50, 51
    warm spinach-artichoke dip,
        40, 41
nuts
    toasting, 257
    see also specific nuts

O

oils, types of, 1–2
olive, kalamata, tapenade, 27
olive oil, about, 2
orange(s)
    Mandarin peanut-crunch
        salad with crispy
        wontons, 58, 59
    orange you glad I made
        crispy tofu?, 181
    -scented cranberry sauce,
        country meatloaf and
        golden gravy with,
        161–64, 162

P

pancakes
  for dinner, *182, 183*
  homemade Chinese, moo
    shu vegetables with, *112,*
    113–14
  keeping hot, 115
parchment paper, 10
pasta
  avocado pesto, *124,* 125
  best-ever macaroni and
    cheese, *126,* 127
  Chinese takeout chow mein,
    128, 129–30
  fettuccine alfredo, *134,* 135
  gluten-free, about, 11
  Italiano, 138
  minted couscous with
    arugula, butternut squash,
    and currants, *60,* 61
  ooh-la-la lasagna, 136–37
  orecchiette in no-cook
    spinach sauce, 131
  penne alla vodka with the
    best garlic bread in the
    world, *142,* 143–44
  salad, easy peasy, *56,* 57
  spaghetti bolognese, 145
  straw and hay, *146,* 147
  stuffed shells with arrabbiata
    sauce, *148,* 149–50
  sweet potato gnocchi with
    sage butter, 151–52, *153*
  wild mushroom stroganoff
    fettuccine, *154,* 155
  see also noodle(s)
pastry doughs, about, 8
peanut butter
  buckeyes, *208,* 209
  dog treats, *246,* 247
  peanutty perfection noodles,
    140, 141
peanut(s)
  -crunch salad, Mandarin,
    with crispy wontons, *58,*
    59
  peanutty perfection noodles,
    140, 141
peas
  Chinese takeout chow mein,
    128, 129–30

easy peasy pasta salad, *56, 57*
Mongolian BBQ seitan, *176,*
  177
pineapple not-so-fried rice,
  184, 185
straw and hay pasta, *146, 147*
teriyaki wok vegetables, 83
peppers
  barley bliss casserole, 158
  jalapeño cornbread poppers
    with whipped maple
    butter, *28,* 29
  tropical island kebabs with
    cilantro rice, *192, 193*–94
pesto
  artichoke-walnut, crostini,
    14, 15
  avocado, pasta, *124, 125*
  pizza, grilled, with sweet
    potatoes, kale, and
    balsamic reduction, 98–99
  portobello, panini, 116
  sauce, 98–99
phyllo
  about, 8
  Moroccan bistilla, *178,*
    179–80
  mushroom turnovers, 36–37
  working with, 37
pies
  Moroccan bistilla, *178,*
    179–80
  summer berry, à la mode,
    235–37, *236*
pineapple
  not-so-fried rice, *184, 185*
  pizza, BBQ, *96,* 97
  salsa, black bean baby cakes
    with, 20–21
  tropical island kebabs with
    cilantro rice, *192, 193*–94
pine nut(s)
  avocado pesto pasta, *124,* 125
  ricotta, rosemary tomato
    galette with, 117–20, *118*
pizza
  BBQ pineapple, *96,* 97
  grilled pesto, with sweet
    potatoes, kale, and
    balsamic reduction, 98–99
pizza dough, basic, 250

plantains, about, 160
plantains and coconut rice,
  Caribbean vegetables
  with, 159–60
potato(es)
  creamy scalloped, thyme for,
    88, 89
  easy peasy pasta salad, *56,*
    57
  guilt-free garlic mashed, 79
  -leek patties, crispy, with
    lemon-dill dip, 22–23
  sea salt and vinegar french
    fries, *86,* 87
  skins, mini, stuffed with
    avocado salsa, *30, 31*–32
  see also sweet potato(es)
puff pastry
  about, 8
  tarte tatin with coconut
    whipped cream, 239–41,
    240
pumpkin
  Chloe's award-winning
    ginger nutmeg spice
    cupcakes, 201–3, *202*

Q

quinoa
  California chipotle chop
    with agave-lime
    vinaigrette, 49

R

raisins
  ooey gooey cinnamon rolls,
    229–31, *230*
  pineapple not-so-fried rice,
    184, 185
  yoga cookies, 245
raspberry sauce, chocolate
  molten lava cakes with,
  212, 213–14
rice
  avocado-shiitake sushi,
    16–17, *17*
  cilantro, tropical island
    kebabs with, *192, 193*–94
  coconut, and plantains,
    Caribbean vegetables
    with, 159–60

rice (*cont.*)
    country meatloaf and golden
      gravy with orange-
      scented cranberry sauce,
      161–64, *162*
    double double drive-thru
      burgers, 103–5, *104*
    Indian buffet trio: saag
      aloo, chana masala, and
      vegetable biryani, with
      garlic naan, 172–75, *174*
    LA-style chimichurri tacos,
      109–11, *110*
    pineapple not-so-fried, *184,*
      185
    sweet-and-sour party
      meatballs, 33–35, *34*
rice milk, about, 7
    rosemary tomato galette
      with pine nut ricotta,
      117–20, *118*

S

sage butter, sweet potato
    gnocchi with, 151–52, *153*
salads
    Caesar, with maple-wheat
      croutons, *46,* 47–48
    California chipotle chop
      with agave-lime
      vinaigrette, 49
    Chloe's favorite five-minute,
      53
    Mandarin peanut-crunch,
      with crispy wontons, *58,*
      59
    minted couscous with
      arugula, butternut
      squash, and currants,
      60, 61
    pasta, easy peasy, *56, 57*
    simple side, with shallot-
      dijon vinaigrette, 62
    wasabi sesame noodle, 68
salt
    about, 4
    sea, and vinegar french fries,
      86, 87
    sea, toffee bars, *232, 233–34*
samosas with cilantro-tamarind
    dipping sauce, 38–39

sandwiches
    avocado toast, *94, 95*
    Chloe's award-winning
      mango masala panini, *100,*
      101–2
    falafel sliders with avocado
      hummus, *106,* 107–8
    portobello pesto panini, 116
    see also burgers
sauces
    barbecue, 254
    marinara, 255
    soy-free soy, 257
    sweet-and-sour, 256
seaweed
    avocado-shiitake sushi,
      16–17, *17*
    under-the-sea vegetables, 92
seitan
    about, 6
    gluten-free substitutes, 12
    homemade, 252
    Mongolian BBQ, *176,* 177
    scallopini, 186
    tropical island kebabs with
      cilantro rice, *192, 193–94*
sesame oil, about, 2
shortening, vegetable, non-
    hydrogenated, about, 2
Silpat, 10
sliders, falafel, with avocado
    hummus, *106,* 107–8
soba noodles, about, 8
soups
    cheesy broccoli, in
      sourdough bread bowls,
      50, 51
    tomato-basil bisque with
      pumpernickel croutons,
      63–65, *64*
    Tuscan bean and greens, over
      garlic toast, 66–67
sour cream, 254
soy-free substitutes, 12
soy milk, about, 7
soy sauce
    gluten-free, about, 12
    soy-free (recipe), 257
    soy-free substitute for, 12
spinach
    -artichoke dip, warm, *40,* 41

green curry crepes, 168–69
Indian buffet trio: saag
    aloo, chana masala, and
    vegetable biryani, with
    garlic naan, 172–75, *174*
ooh-la-la lasagna, 136–37
sauce, no-cook, orecchiette
    in, 131
squash
    butternut, arugula, and
      currants, minted
      couscous with, *60, 61*
    Chloe's award-winning
      ginger nutmeg spice
      cupcakes, 201–3, *202*
    lentil, and apple stew,
      curried, *54, 55*
    teriyaki wok vegetables, 83
    stew, curried lentil, squash,
      and apple, *54, 55*
sugar, vegan, buying, 8–9
sushi, avocado-shiitake, 16–17,
    17
sweeteners, types of, 8–9
sweet potato(es)
    Caribbean vegetables
      with coconut rice and
      plantains, 159–60
    gnocchi with sage butter,
      151–52, *153*
    kale, and balsamic reduction,
      grilled pesto pizza with,
      98–99

T

tacos, LA-style chimichurri,
    109–11, *110*
tahini
    about, 4
    falafel sliders with avocado
      hummus, *106,* 107–8
tamarind-cilantro dipping sauce,
    samosas with, 38–39
tapenade, kalamata olive, 27
tarts
    rosemary tomato galette
      with pine nut ricotta,
      117–20, *118*
    tarte tatin with coconut
      whipped cream, 239–41,
      240

tempeh
about, 6
country meatloaf and golden gravy with orange-scented cranberry sauce, 161–64, *162*
double double drive-thru burgers, 103–5, *104*
piccata, *190*, 191
soy-free substitutes for, 12
sweet-and-sour party meatballs, 33–35, *34*
tempura, vegetable, *90*, 91
teriyaki wok vegetables, 83
Thai chickpea burgers with sweet 'n' spicy sauce, 121–22
thickeners, types of, 9
thyme for creamy scalloped potatoes, 88, 89
tofu
about, 6
BBQ pineapple pizza, *96*, 97
Caesar salad with maple-wheat croutons, *46*, 47–48
crispy potato-leek patties with lemon-dill dip, 22–23
double double drive-thru burgers, 103–5, *104*
moo shu vegetables with homemade Chinese pancakes, *112*, 113–14
Moroccan bistilla, *178*, 179–80
ooh-la-la lasagna, 136–37
orange you glad I made crispy tofu?, 181
pineapple not-so-fried rice, *184*, 185
pressing, 252
sour cream, 254

soy-free substitutes for, 12
stuffed shells with arrabbiata sauce, *148*, 149–50
warm spinach-artichoke dip, *40*, 41
tomato(es)
balsamic bruschetta, 19
barley bliss casserole, 158
-basil bisque with pumpernickel croutons, 63–65, *64*
galette, rosemary, with pine nut ricotta, 117–20, *118*
ketchup, sweet, 253
marinara sauce, 255
penne alla vodka with the best garlic bread in the world, *142*, 143–44
stuffed shells with arrabbiata sauce, *148*, 149–50
tortillas
keeping hot, 115
LA-style chimichurri tacos, 109–11, *110*
truffles, *242*, 243
turnovers, phyllo mushroom, 36–37

U
udon noodles, about, 8

V
vanilla bean ice cream, 238
vegetable(s)
Caribbean, with coconut rice and plantains, 159–60
classic roasted, 71
cutting in chiffonade, 77
Indian buffet trio: saag aloo, chana masala, and vegetable biryani, with garlic naan, 172–75, *174*

moo shu, with homemade Chinese pancakes, *112*, 113–14
tempura, *90*, 91
teriyaki wok, 83
under-the-sea, 92
see also specific vegetables
vegetable shortening, non-hydrogenated, about, 2
vinegar, 9
vital wheat gluten
homemade seitan, 252
Vitamix, 10
vodka, penne alla, with the best garlic bread in the world, *142*, 143–44

W
walnut(s)
-artichoke pesto crostini, *14*, 15
double double drive-thru burgers, 103–5, *104*
fudge, chocolate, *218*, 219
iced apple cake squares, 225
spaghetti bolognese, 145
sweet-and-sour party meatballs, 33–35, *34*
yoga cookies, 245
wasabi sesame noodle salad, 68
wheat flour, about, *5*
wontons
with apricot-mustard sauce, *42*, 43–44
crispy, Mandarin peanut-crunch salad with, *58*, 59

X
xanthan gum, about, 9

Y
yams, coconut mashed, with currants, *72*, 73
yoga cookies, 245

About the Author

Chef Chloe Coscarelli is a Food Network–winning vegan chef, proving to the world that vegan food can be stylish, delicious, and easy. She took home first place on Food Network's *Cupcake Wars*, making her the first vegan ever to win on a Food Network competition. Chloe is a graduate of The Natural Gourmet Institute of Health and Culinary Arts NYC; the University of California, Berkeley; as well as Cornell University's Plant-Based Nutrition Program by Dr. T. Colin Campbell (The China Study). Additional work includes Millennium Restaurant San Francisco, Counter Organic Vegetarian Bistro New York City, and Herbivore Restaurant Berkeley. Chloe is a *VegNews* and *New York Times* contributor. To learn more about Chloe, join her community at ChefChloe.com.